# THE KEY OF DAVID

*Tall Pine Books: Where Your Purpose Meets Print*
|| tallpinebooks.com

# THE KEY OF DAVID

EXPERIENCING THE VOICE OF GOD

DAVID CUPPETT

Tall Pine

## ENDORSEMENTS

"David Cuppett is a close friend of ours. He is a man of deep passion for the Lord and the Church. David speaks a revelatory language much like Isaiah, Ezekiel and John. He is able to discern and interpret his dreams and visions from the Spirit of the Lord and release the words to the body or an individual to bring them into a place of deliverance and awakening. He brings forth the anointing to introduce people to the living God.

*The Key of David* contains more than good principles. It is an invitation to bring you into a deeper relationship with Holy Spirit as He reveals Christ in you and through you. This book may challenge you in many ways. If you allow God to speak to you as you read, it will revolutionize how you see yourself in Christ. You will be awakened to the voice of Holy Spirit in your life and truly be filled with the power from on high."

—**Steve and Tabby Wollard**
Senior Pastors *The Well Ministries*,
Newark, OH

"In a time where ministers, the church, and believers need to be empowered by the Spirit of God this book is a true blessing. David has experienced the power of the Holy Spirit in a way that so many people only hear about. God has given him the understanding of the need, the purpose, and the ability of how to build a relationship with the Holy Spirit. This relationship is life transforming and empowers you to fulfill your destiny in the kingdom of God.

In this book David shares his story and shows us how to encounter and fellowship with the Holy Spirit in an intimate way and how to live a Spirit lead and empowered life. It's more than just religion and it's more than just being saved. There is a personal relationship. God has given David an understanding and revelation in how to walk into the Spirit-filled life that Jesus told us about. This is a must read that you will love. You must experience this book!"

—**Jonothan and Jennifer Ables**
Senior Pastors *Victory Church*,
El Dorado, Arkanas and Gulf Shores, Alabama

# CONTENTS

# FOREWORD

We are so overwhelmed to share our recent experiences with the Holy spirit. Prophet David has been called by God to bring great change to me and my dear wife Lydia through the dreams and visions that sent him to us and the churches of our region. The vision of the Lord that sent David to me and our people, which has brought great spiritual power into our lives. Through our new relationship over the past twelve months, I have personally encountered the Holy spirit and have heard the voice of God. His voice has changed my life and purpose.

As a result of this connection to David and 5 Stones Ministries, hundreds of pastors in this region of India, along with thousands of believers, have encountered the Holy Spirit which is a great miracle. Many of us have seen visions and prophesied for the first time ever just like the book of Acts. Since the awakening of the spiritual gifts in our pastors, we asked David to lead us deeper and write about the Holy Spirit for us to explain what it means to listen for the Holy Spirit's voice and follow Him.

As a result, David sent us this book which has touched my heart, bringing understanding and clear vision for my ministry in India, equipping those around me to hear the voice of God. Many changes have been taking place in our life and ministry over the last twelve months since we met David and encountered the Holy Spirit. Our meetings are now places where miracle power of the Holy Spirit is expected by the people. We now know that Jesus is the God of victory in spirit, body and soul.

This book will awaken deep love for the Holy Spirit and a life which expects in His great power to lead us through life. Our prayer is that all who read this book will have the same encounters and transformation that we have had in India.

—**Joshua and Lydia Bandlamudi**
Senior Pastors, *Five Stones Ministries*
India

# INTRODUCTION

## WILL YOU SPEAK FOR ME?

Isaiah 6:8 "Whom shall I send, and who will go for Us?"

It is funny how life works out sometimes, unable to see what is ahead, we often are a victim of the world and its consuming nature, no matter how hard we work or where we come from. However, that is not the view of the Holy Spirit. There is a destiny which the Lord has written of us, that is an opportunity to step out of the boundaries of this world and the limitations it places upon us, as well as the definition of what *success* is (Hebrews 10:7). But most importantly, this destiny that is written of us in the volumes of books in heaven, holds the answers to the questions that are deep inside of everybody born into this world; *who am I and what is my purpose?*

I thought I had made it in the early 90's, being the first on my father's side to go to college and graduate with a degree. The world was mine, so I thought, but what I found is that a degree was just a different kind of confinement. It seemed normal to be limited in finances and not really have any extra, other than what was needed to eat and keep a roof over my head. My degree was going to change that, or so I thought. I found when I entered the professional work environment within the chemical industry, that the pressures of succeeding were, in ways, heavier than not having anything. By the time I entered my early thirties, my wife and I had lived in seven different cities, never really able to connect with the community before it was time to take on a bigger responsibility and take the next promotion that was being offered. These advancements in the corporate world felt like I had sold my soul. I had international responsibilities in chemical operations, and I was supposed to be enjoying the fruits of hard work, but I found that hard work could not fill that void I felt in my soul. So, I bought motorcycles and started doing adventurous things including riding that motorcycle at light speed, jeopardizing me and the people around me so I could momentarily fill that void in my soul with enough excitement to feel like I was alive. When I wasn't riding at the speed of light, I was drinking, trying to drown the pain that I was feeling deep in my soul. Basic questions were continual in my mind: is this it? Is this all the world has to offer? Is this what I was born to do?

I grew up with parents who loved me and took me to a local denominational church. It was a place that talked about Jesus, and the people cared for each other, but I never saw the power of God. I can remember thinking as a child that I didn't know the difference [8]between Santa Claus, the Easter Bunny and Jesus. So, through my early twenties and into my thirties, I walked alone. There was no religion in my life. As this time of climbing the corporate ladder was taking its toll on my soul, I turned to adrenaline and alcohol trying to fill that void or numb the pain. I finally got to a point of breaking in the spring of 2005. I was sitting in my car contemplating many things and I said *"Jesus, if you are real, you better come quick because I'm about to check out of this place!"*

Several weeks later, my sister-in-law invited my wife and I to come to a church and hear a missionary speak. I reluctantly said yes, but we purposely waited to walk in late because I didn't want to sit in worship. We came in and snuck into the back row, not wanting to be seen. All I wanted to do is listen to this guy, appease my sister-in-law, and then go home. However, I didn't know that this one night was going to change my life forever.

The worship stopped and the missionary was introduced at the pulpit. He started to preach, and it sounded like nothing I had ever heard before. It was powerful and with authority. This was not a powerless pastor who just went through the motions. This was somebody who spoke with purpose and intent. I was intrigued to say the least. Suddenly, about fifteen minutes into his message, he stopped and paused, looking in the direction where I was sitting. He jumped down off the stage and started walking down the aisle toward the back of the church. He walked all the way back to where I was sitting, and stood in front of me. He pointed at me and started to speak saying *"Son, the Holy Spirit has a plan for your life, and He wants an answer from you now! Will you let me pray for you?"*

I answered before I could think. It was like something inside of me that was waiting to get identified, answering the question, *"YES!"* I said and stood up. My knees were shaking. The hair on my arms stood up. There was a presence I never felt before. I followed him to the front of church. He started to say he saw me in a vision leading an army, and that I would teach them to drink water in a way that would make them mighty! He said, *"You are a Gideon who has been hiding in a wine cellar, doing the wrong thing in the wrong place, but today the Holy Spirit is here to clothe you in power. You will one day awaken the army of the Lord Jesus Christ to drink of the living water of the Holy Spirit!"* He then laid his hand on my head and asked me a question. He asked, *"Do you pray in tongues and do you know the Holy Spirit?"* I said, *"No, I don't even know what tongues are. What are tongues?"* He chuckled and said *"Receive the Holy Spirit!"*

My wife said I fell to the ground and laid there motionless. The missionary got back on stage and started preaching again for some time. She said that after about thirty minutes, I rolled over. I remember standing up and feeling this fire in my belly. Suddenly this prayer language, they called tongues, started flowing out of my mouth. I couldn't stop praying in tongues. I was shaking and praying in tongues for hours following the service. Little did I know, this was just the beginning of the unveiling of the destiny that Jesus had for me. I shook the whole way home as my wife drove, tongues still flowing out of my mouth.

My wife ended up going to sleep, but I could not. My whole world just got turned upside down. I went over to a spare room and sat on the bed. Immediately, I heard the voice of Jesus Christ for the first time in my life. He kept telling me, *"It's ok!"* while I sat there and confessed every wrong thing I did in my life. All He would say is, *"It's ok!"* Suddenly, around 2 a.m., He started asking me a question, *"Will you speak for Me?"* I answered with every excuse I could think of including, *"I do not know your Bible, I am unworthy, I am afraid to speak in front of crowds,* etc." He would come back every fifteen minutes with the same question, *"Will you speak for Me?"*

At approximately 6 a.m., with the hair on my arms still standing up and my body shaking in the presence of the Holy Spirit, He came again and asked, *"Will you speak for Me?"* At this point, after an all-night debate, I decided to cut Him a deal. I said, *"Ok, I'll speak if I am asked, but don't expect me to volunteer!"* Something shifted in that moment. He got what He came to get, which was my heart's commitment to do what He would ask me to do. I felt a shift in the room. It was now early Sunday morning and I was so awake and on fire in the Holy Spirit, I got dressed and went downstairs to eat breakfast and hear my wife's perspective of what happened. I got downstairs and she said, *"I think we should go back to that church this morning to hear that guy again. By the way, how do you feel after what happened to you last night?"* I played it off like it was no big deal. I certainly wasn't going to tell her that Jesus spoke to me all night long because, let's be real, neither of us ever heard of Jesus Himself speaking to people and I certainly was not ready to tell what happened when she went to sleep.

So, we get in the car and drive to this church, go in and find a seat. After worship, the missionary begins his message. However, just like the previous night, he stops and looks in the direction of where I am sitting. He gets down from the pulpit and walks down the aisle. He then puts the mic in front of me and says, *"The Spirit of God told me that you would speak if you were asked so I'm asking you to speak for Jesus!"* I felt this supernatural equipping energy come down over me. It removed every fear and inhibition as the missionary led me to the front of the church. I could feel this fire in my belly and suddenly these words testifying of Jesus Christ Himself speaking to me all night long came out of my mouth. The next thing I know the altar was filled with people who wanted to hear the voice of God. People came forward weeping and seeking the Holy Spirit. It was the beginning of a supernatural life and a life where that void no longer ruled my soul. Within weeks, I was leading prayer ministry and supernatural things like casting out demons, prophecy and miracles were happening when I prayed.

From this point forward, the void that ruled my soul was filled and my purpose was made clear; *awaken the army of the Lord to the living waters of His voice!*

## 1

## THE PROMISE OF THE FATHER: I WILL MAKE YOU A HOUSE

### HEAVEN INVADES EARTH

2 Samuel 7:11 "Also the Lord tells you that He will make you a house."

WHEN I WAS GROWING UP, THE CONCEPT OF *JESUS* AND *HEAVEN* were merely things that were talked about in church. I don't recall ever seeing a miracle or anything else that would indicate to me that heaven invades earth. Heaven was a concept I understood as a place you may go at the end of your life, but I had no proof of it being real. However, a few months following the experience I described in the Introduction of this book, strange things started happening.

I was minding my own business, helping my wife on a Saturday morning by taking my two-year-old son and my three-year-old daughter to McDonald's so that my wife could have a break. We go in and get our pancakes and watch them shove as much food as possible down their throats as fast as they can so they can go play. After all, that is why we go to McDonald's right? Little did I know something wild was about to happen as they ran over to the climbing station.

There were five moms huddled together talking while their kids were playing. I sat there alone watching for a few moments and then decided to pull out my Bible. I had been reading the Psalms so I turned the page to Psalm 27. I began reading and made it to verse 4 which reads in the NIV: *"One thing I ask from the Lord, this only do I seek: that I may dwell in the house of the Lord all the days of my life, to gaze on the beauty of the Lord and to seek him in his temple."* As I was reading verse 4, I started feeling this heat over the top of my head and oil appeared on my face to such a degree that it was dripping onto the table. I was in shock!

It continued to drip onto my Bible from my face, the Spirit of God was falling upon me so powerfully. I started to shake and weep uncontrollably. It was like the Holy Spirit was doing heart surgery right there in the middle of McDonald's. I tried to keep myself together, after all there were other people in the room. Nevertheless, the oil kept dripping and tears started flowing harder and harder. I continued shaking, so overwhelmed by the Holy Spirit that I slid off the chair onto the floor, weeping uncontrollably. This continued for a few minutes. I lost total awareness of who else was in the room or even that I was in a public place. The Spirit of God chose that moment to reveal Himself in such a powerful way that it would be witnessed. I suddenly hear a woman saying "Sir, sir, are you ok? What is wrong? Can we help you?" Still weeping and shaking, the best I can do at this point is lift my arm and point to the Bible.

The only words that I got out of my mouth were "The Holy Spirit is real! The Holy Spirit is real!" All the children in

McDonald's suddenly became aware of their moms standing around me as I sat on the floor. So now all the moms and children are staring at me! I remember my three-year-old daughter Kami looking at me and pulling out her pacifier saying, "Are you OK Dad?" A peace filled the room; then there was silence. The faces of the moms looked like they were in shock. They knew something was in the room; they could feel it. And still, the only words that came out of my mouth were, "The Holy Spirit is real!" Everybody, including the children sat or stood in silence. The spiritual presence of the Lord invaded McDonald's and everybody knew it. We continued in silence, in absolute awe of the presence of God invading McDonald's. After about twenty minutes of complete silence and awe, I was able to stand up and pull myself together. I gathered my kids and my Bible and made it home soon after, but all I could do was weep. The Holy Spirit spoke to me the night I was baptized in the Holy Spirit, but this was a whole new level. Heaven invaded earth, releasing oil that appeared out of thin air.

Something happened to my heart that day. The words on paper, the Bible, literally came alive and heaven revealed itself. His world invaded my world. His equipping oil ran down my face in a public place. His Spirit became more real and overpowering than the Bible itself. The force called the Holy Spirit made Himself known in such a way that I now know that this world does not limit Him. Not only that, but this heart that King David expressed, was in absolute love with the Holy Spirit. And the Holy Spirit was in absolute love with David. I learned what made David great, invincible to the natural world. It was this love affair with the Spirit of God who invaded the earth everywhere David went. It is the One they call the Holy Spirit who does the impossible.

## THE MAKING OF KINGS

The heart of David is something the Lord Jesus Christ magnifies as the intent of God through the story of the restoration of man. This restoration is something that man cannot do alone, nor does he possess the power through his own will and decision making to achieve this righteousness. Righteousness is a gift that can only be *imparted* and it operates *from the inside out.* Transformation is the work of the One who raised Christ from the dead. The One they call the Holy Spirit. The result of this gift of righteousness is a heart and soul that emulates the very heart of God Himself. The ability to love. This is the grace of restoration and the design of the Lord to rescue mankind from the depths of darkness and the tomb of death. Heart surgery is performed by Him to a degree that love is dominant and forceful, invading the darkness of the heart around us, even to the degree that supernatural things happen because of this love.

David was chosen by the Lord Jesus Christ from the womb, even though David was born in iniquity (Psalm 51:5). Like all of us who are trapped in this dark world from birth, the plan of the Lord is magnificent. David was the least of his brothers, but was the one the Lord sought out when Samuel was sent to anoint David with the Holy Spirit (1 Samuel 16:1-13). The Holy Spirit initially equipped David with supernatural ability and a heart to follow the Spirit of God into the unknown. This included impossible feats, such as defeating a giant named Goliath. But the greatest work of all was the transformation of David's soul and heart through a season of being alone with the Holy Spirit.

In David's period of running from Saul and surviving his time in the desert, the Holy Spirit fashioned David's heart so that by the time David was made king (fulfilling the prophecy spoken of by the Prophet Samuel) David's heart and soul were transformed by such a deep caring love for God Himself, that David's concern when he was made king was for God alone. David spent so much time depending upon the Spirit of God, between the time of killing the giant and being positioned by the Spirit to sit on the throne, that his whole focus was upon God. This love is what produced *Psalm 27:4 NIV, "One thing I ask from the Lord, this only do I seek: that I may dwell in the house of the Lord all the days of my life, to gaze on the beauty of the Lord and to seek him in his temple."*

In 2 Samuel 7:1-17, David and Nathan the prophet are sitting in the beautiful palace where God positioned David. David's heart for God was so tender by this time, that he was concerned that God did not have a dwelling place since the Ark was taken out of the Tabernacle of Moses. David declared to Nathan, *"I will build the Lord a house to dwell in!"* Nathan, as a friend said, *"What a great idea, go for it!"* Later that night, God woke up Nathan and spoke to him (as a prophet) about David's intent to build Him a house and how it so touched God's heart. God declared three amazing promises to David. These promises included first that David's descendants would sit on thrones ruling forever, secondly that God Himself would be an enemy to David's enemies and third; that God would make David and his descendants a house of the Lord Himself, meaning that the presence of God would dwell with David.

David's heart for God gave him supernatural ability. Love for God produced the supernatural. David discerned through love what the Lord was actually saying to Nathan, which was that God would no longer look to dwell in a building or location such as where the Ark of the Covenant was placed in the old covenant, but the Lord was prophesying that He would put a tabernacle in the heart of David and the river of life would flow from that place. The oil would flow. This is a promise to David and the descendants of David. David immediately took the Ark of the Covenant to Zion upon hearing what the Lord said to Nathan, placing the Ark (the Presence) in the Tent of David.

David realizes he has access to the presence of the Lord Himself (the very heart of God) and it was granted to Him. David dwells in this place next to the Ark, able to be so close with the Lord that the river of life from the Lord's heart continuously flows out of David's mouth (heart). David is granted access to the presence of the Lord like no other. That was in a time under the old covenant Law, where the only people that had access to the Ark, were the high priests of the Levite tribe and even then, the only way to enter the Holy of Holies was through the ritual practice of bringing the blood of the sacrifice (Hebrews 9:25, Leviticus 3:8). According to the Law of Moses, David should have been struck dead based on the law and how the Law of Moses was demonstrated to the Levite priests who entered the Holy of Holies without blood. How could this be? What was unique about David? Why could he actually lay next to the Ark (Psalm 17:8, 57:1) without being struck dead by the Holiness of God?

## ACCESS TO THE HEART OF GOD AND THE SUPERNATURAL POWER OF THE HOLY SPIRIT

The Bible says that David functioned under a different law. The Israelites who surrounded David were bound by the Law of Moses, without ever being able to have their conscious cleansed, healing their broken souls and evil hearts. David functioned out of a different law which transformed his heart and soul. David was bound to the Holy Spirit whereas the Levite priest and the nation of Israel was bound to a covenant of death, the Law of Moses (2 Corinthians 3:7, Hebrews 9:6-9). David's renewed heart and soul had access to the law of the Spirit. While the Pharisees and Sadducees led the rituals of the covenant of death, David dwelled in the presence of the Lord and the prophecies and psalms flowed out of David's heart. The voice of God was heard and inscribed on earth through a man who was not bound to death (Law of Moses – old covenant), but was bound to the life giving power of the Spirit of God. David himself prophetically reveals the contrast between these two different laws.

*Psalm 1:1-6, "Blessed is the man who walks not in the counsel of the ungodly, Nor stands in the path of sinners, Nor sits in the seat of the scornful; But his delight is in the law of the Lord, and in His law he meditates day and night. He shall be like a tree planted by the rivers of water, that brings forth its fruit in its season, whose leaf also shall not wither; And whatever he does shall prosper. The ungodly are not so, but are like the chaff which the wind drives away. Therefore the ungodly shall not stand in the judgment, Nor sinners in the congregation of the righteous. For the Lord knows the way of the righteous, But the way of the ungodly shall perish."*

In verse 2, the prophecy reveals the *law of the Lord* is where the one who prospers will dwell and he will overcome. The word *law* in this context is related to verse 3 which states that *he* will be planted by the river. There are two levels of meaning (or two dimensions) to the word *law* (**Torah**). The first level, or dimension, is the most common understanding of the Torah and is known as the Law of Moses (the Ten Commandments) or the scripture which is visible and able to be followed ritually. It is the scripture which people recognize as the breathed word God documented on paper (or stone tablets).

However, you must realize, the Ten Commandments and the

rituals of the Law of Moses were actually given to Moses for the nation of Israel because they refused to ascend the mountain when Moses was sent down to invite them up (Exodus 20 and 34). As a result, the nation received the intent and design of the rituals of the Law of Moses, instead of the spirit to Spirit (face-to-face) connection the Lord offered. They refused the face of God, and consequently their hearts chose for them to see God on paper. This is not the original intent of the Lord who wanted to know His people face to face. However, it was a mirror, a reflection of the condition of their heart. They needed a savior, but they were not transparent in heart, able to see His face. Instead they were relegated to knowing God only through writings and periodic experiences where Moses was the access point to the supernatural. But God began weaving His plan for all to dwell in a face-to-face relationship with Him in the supernatural realm of the Holy Spirit.

The spirit of the Torah has an underlying meaning that is revealed as the foundation of God's original intent in inviting the nation of Israel up the mountain. The root word of Torah is the word *Yarah* which means "to flow as a river." Imagine that, Psalm 2:3 reveals the way of victory and overcoming is not by ritual and working to achieve adherence to the Law of Moses, but through the flow of the Holy Spirit. Hearts are only changed through the resurrection power of the Spirit. Man does not possess the ability to change his own heart by simply making a decision. Only the Spirit can resurrect.

This flow of the Holy Spirit (the speaking voice and the direct contact with the Spirit) revealed David's path and God's intent. David's heart was transformed by the Spirit and the voice of God was manifest resulting in psalms, prophecies and spiritual songs flowing not only from David's heart, but from the people who followed David to the tent where he lay in the shadow of the Almighty and the Spirit spoke. This is the river of the Holy Spirit, the water gate pouring out to all, opening the heart to the Spirit of God imparting dreams, visions and prophecies. David produced an atmosphere of life because of the Holy Spirit. The relationship of love was so deep that God and David declared over each other saying, *I will build you a house!* They sought to dwell together in the Spirit. Imagine that, the gifts of the Holy Spirit functioned in a time where the Law of Moses should have brought David death.

## THE PROMISE

The coming promise of the Holy Spirit in the new covenant reveals the very contrast between the old covenant and the new covenant. *Romans 8:2, For the law of the Spirit of life in Christ Jesus has made me free from the law of sin and death.*

The revelation of the Spirit of God is profound and life changing. The Holy Spirit, through Paul, reveals the vast contrast between the old and the new saying that there are two laws. One law binds you to death while the other law binds you to life. Only in the death of the old, can one receive the life of the new. A mind (soul) given to love the Holy Spirit with all your heart crying out for the Spirit of God to flow through your soul allows the voice of God to speak, releasing light into the darkness and where light is released, the darkness cannot withstand the light (John 1:1-5). Light always wins! Love never fails!

This new paradigm that David revealed in the time of the covenant of death, was prophesied to be offered to all of humanity. In Isaiah 22:22 it is prophesied that "The messiah would carry the key of David on His shoulder," indicating that the authority of access to the heart of God would be granted through the coming Christ, the Messiah who restores man to life in the Spirit of God which was stolen all the way back in the garden of Eden. In Amos 9:11 it is prophesied that God would restore David's fallen tent which is the place where God spoke in visions, dreams and face to face encounters. This is the intent of the Spirit, to restore life with God Himself. This is confirmed in Isaiah 2:3 which is a prophecy that says *"the Law (**Yarah** – flow of the Spirit) shall come forth out of Zion, the place of David's tent"* – no other than David's heart. This place is ultimately the heart of sons and daughters who embrace this love affair to the degree that love produces psalms, songs, prophecies and all the gifts of the Spirit (the means in which God speaks). God Himself said He is in no need of a house, but desires to flow out of the heart of men (2 Samuel 7:1-17).

Jesus Christ is revealed in Revelation 3:7 as *He who has the key of David, He who opens and no one shuts, and shuts and no one opens.* The concept of *doors* is a means of access to the dimension of the Spirit through the Holy Spirit. When Jesus appeared on the scene at the river Jordan, He was baptized in the Holy Spirit and then demonstrated the heart of David. Repeatedly through the four gospels, it is said that Jesus went to be alone with the Spirit (His Father). In prayer, Jesus heard the Spirit who gave visions, dreams and face to face encounters revealing the mission for the next day and every situation in which Jesus found Himself. He was led by the Spirit to the woman at the well, led by the Spirit to the man at the country of the Gadarenes, He was led by the Spirit to feed the five thousand. Everything Jesus did was through the flow (*Yarah*) of the Holy Spirit (the law of the Spirit) who spoke and released heaven on earth, just like David. Jesus, the Son of David (Matthew 1:1) shook the earth through the flow of the Spirit.

Jesus demonstrated life in the Spirit as the Son of David, delighting in the constant flow of the Spirit, releasing heaven on earth every day. But when it was time to multiply and take His seat at the right hand of the Father, Jesus started His path to the cross because the cross would be the way in which the old covenant was fulfilled and the new covenant would be made manifest (see Hebrews 9 and 10). In this new covenant, Jesus would give the Spirit of God to the masses, fulfilling the promise made to David. All believers could receive the promises made to David.

When Jesus took His last breath on the cross and said, *It is finished,* He fulfilled the Law of Moses (Matthew 5:17-20) making this way of living obsolete. He descended into hell and took the keys of death and hades (Revelation 1:18) so now all authority has been given to Him (Matthew 28:18). This authority is the manifestation of the prophecy to David as King, his descendants would sit on thrones and rule over the dark powers of the earth, having conquered them through Christ. And just as Jesus was faithful unto death, depending on the Holy Spirit to resurrect Him from the dead, the Holy Spirit would be sent to all of mankind to resurrect men from the tomb of the covenant of death (the Law of Moses).

Instead of being bound to the dimension of the earth, the Spirit of God would grant access to the heart of God and the flow of the Spirit. No longer would people be bound to ritual worship, but to the moving of the Spirit. All men who receive life, would receive it as a gift through the One who holds all keys and chose to send one thing, the power of the Holy Spirit who would center men's hearts around the Spirit of God and not the dead words on paper that were designed to reveal the need of a living savior.

Jesus sent the Spirit as the One who fulfills the renewing of the heart. It is the Spirit of God who writes on the heart, transforming it into flesh, sensitive and giving the ability to hear the living voice, the flow of the Spirit, resurrecting men and women from the dead (Ezekiel 36:26, John 3:2-8). No longer would the Spirit of God be held behind curtains and be accessible to only the religious elite of Israel, but instead the lost, the broken, the weak and those who have no strength would be given access to King Jesus and they would also be made to sit upon thrones as descendants of the Son of David.

# 2

# THE SALT COVENANT

## RESURRECTION POWER

Acts 1:8 "And you shall receive power when the Holy Spirit comes upon you and you shall be my witnesses..."

THE RESURRECTION OF JESUS CHRIST IS AN AMAZING PICTURE OF the absolute dependence Jesus had in trusting the Holy Spirit. The plan of resurrection was not just dependent upon Jesus following through with the prophecies of crushing the head of the serpent (Genesis 3:15) by taking sin and death to the grave, but the Holy Spirit's ability to raise Jesus from the dead was as important as the work of Jesus. Without the work of the Holy Spirit, the accomplishment of Christ on the cross is left unvalidated, rendering man still ill-equipped.

The trust of Jesus, the Son of David, to willingly take the covenant of death (the Law of Moses) to the grave, was a trust and expectancy in the Holy Spirit for His own life, let alone the life of man. The serpent (sin) was hung on the cross (2 Corinthians 5:21; Galatians 3:13), but He was absolutely dependent on the Holy Spirit to finish the work. Death is conquered by the Spirit. Jesus did His job, living a perfect life by following the voice of the Spirit even to the cross. And now, He would have to trust the Spirit to the degree that only the Spirit of God could fulfill the prophecies of resurrection. The Holy Spirit orchestrated the whole thing. He led Jesus into death and then rolled away the stone when Jesus ascended out of hell holding all keys of authority (the keys of life and death – Revelation 1:18).

Jesus trusted and depended on the Spirit for resurrection. This is the way of the Spirit, which is in deep contrast with the way of the Law of Moses. No matter how hard man works to follow the Ten Commandments, he cannot achieve what only Jesus Christ could achieve as the mediator of the new covenant (Hebrews 7) and the Holy Spirit who positioned Jesus in victory. The value of the Holy Spirit is so great that the Spirit alone is the gift Jesus gave to the world (Acts 2:1-4). He commanded us to *love* in the new covenant, equipping all with the power to do so. Without the Spirit of God, it is impossible to love supernaturally. Love is the only fruit of the Spirit that produces in the heart of man: kindness, gentleness, joy, peace, endurance, faithfulness, and self-control. The same Spirit that equipped David to love God with all his heart, all his mind and all his soul, was the very gift Jesus sent to the world.

When Jesus ascended out of Hell holding all authority and all power, He told the disciples and the hundreds of believers, to wait in the city until He sent the Promise of the Father (Luke 24:49). This promise is the promise made to David in 2 Samuel 7:1-13, which would result in David's descendants in the Spirit being transformed into *Houses of the Living God!* This dwelling of the presence of God would resurrect the soul and the heart of man in a way that the Law of Moses could not do. The presence of God would be an enemy to your enemies and establish your authority on the thrones promised to sons and daughters of God. This is a work of the Holy Spirit.

## THE GIFT OF POWER THAT TRANSFORMS

As Jesus was instructing the crowd before He ascended to heaven as to the coming of the promise of the Father, He gave further detail in *Acts 1:8, And you shall receive power and you shall be My witnesses...* In this context, Jesus is revealing how the believer is made the house of God, the design of the new covenant where God tabernacles with man. The power that is referenced here has two implications. First, His presence would be the fulfilling factor of warring against all things that come against you as a new child of God who houses God Himself. Second, is the fact that the Promise (the Holy Spirit) is the One who does the work. The Spirit of God would do what man could not do by working to achieve the scriptures. The Spirit Himself would transform the heart and soul of sons and daughters. The word *power* in Acts 1:8 is the Greek word **Dunamis** meaning *to transform the soul, to renew the heart, to make His dwelling place.*

The greatest theological mistake today is for a person to come to the altar and say, *I believe in Christ,* yet continue in *trying to do it alone.* Resurrection is a work of the Spirit, not man. To neglect the power of the Holy Spirit is like trying to start your car without the key. In every form of Holy Spirit neglect, Christians typically revert back to some twisted form of self-promoting attempts to achieve the Law of Moses. The greatest

Christians are not those who have an appearance of holiness, but those in absolute dependence upon the Holy Spirit who imputes righteousness immediately (Romans 4:11), but then also continuously roots out darkness from the soul and writes His *Yarah* on the hearts of sons and daughters of God by speaking directly to the heart (more to come in later chapters on this topic). Jesus said in John 7:38 that the living waters of the Holy Spirit would flow out of the heart of men and women who receive the Spirit of God. Those who learn to walk according to the Spirit, listening for the flowing voice of God, these are the sons of God; the sons of David and the promises granted through Christ (Romans 8:5).

## THE FULLNESS OF HIS MISSION WAS TO EQUIP YOU WITH THE HOLY SPIRIT

Jesus was so adamant about fulfilling His mission through the cross in order to send the Holy Spirit, that He said, *"It is to your advantage that I go away so that I may send you the Holy Spirit" John 16:7.* Jesus knew that the sooner He accomplished His mission of taking the sin of man to the grave, the sooner the new covenant containing the *Dunamis* power necessary to cleanse the conscience of man (Hebrews 9:13-14) could be sent from heaven to earth. Until that time, the old covenant was in effect and man was subject fully to the darkness of the age. But just as Jesus was resurrected, so too would man be resurrected by the Holy Spirit, doing what the Ten Commandments and the Law of Moses could never do.

Jesus touted the Holy Spirit as being the One who would execute the three promises made to David in the Davidic covenant (also known as the Covenant of Salt – 2 Chronicles 13:5) as we discussed in the previous chapter. This Salt Covenant is portrayed by Jesus in *John 16:7-11, "Nevertheless I tell you the truth. It is to your advantage that I go away; for if I do not go away, the Helper will not come to you; but if I depart, I will send Him to you. And when He has come, He will convict the world of sin, of right-eousness, and of judgment: of sin, because they do not believe in Me; of righteousness, because I go to My Father and you see Me no more; of judgment, because the ruler of this world is judged."*

We will break down the value of each of these three promises and connect them with the promises of the Davidic covenant. It is necessary that every believer see the value of the Holy Spirit and makes the Holy Spirit the necessity that Jesus magnified as the One who would complete the mission; mean-ing, not just the victory at the cross, but the resurrection. Just as the Holy Spirit raised Christ from the dead, the Holy Spirit came to resurrect men from being entombed by this world to the covenant of death.

The command of Jesus in Acts 1:4 when He said, *stay in this city until I send the Holy Spirit and you shall receive power* (*Dunamis*), is not a *bolt-on option*, like the decision of getting a car with air-conditioning. Air conditioning in a car is a true option because you could live with it or without it. However, the Holy Spirit in not a *bolt-on option*. The Holy Spirit is the centerpiece of the *Salt Covenant* and the only means by which a person is resur-rected to life. Altars were never meant to be places of decision. Altars of the Lord are a place of face-to-face encounter where the Holy Spirit does the heart surgery and the transforming work of God.

To understand the intent of *dunamis* power in your life and the intent of the Holy Spirit, you must recognize His vision for your life. This is eloquently portrayed in Isaiah 61 where the

Lord declares His view of those He comes to rescue from this dark world. Again, the three promises of the Salt Covenant are intertwined in the mission of the Holy Spirit in your life. He worked a supernatural feat on the cross, but even more so, He sent the Holy Spirit to unveil your heavenly identity through the full manifestation of these three promises of the Salt Covenant.

*Isaiah 61:1-3 (AMP) "The Spirit of the Lord God is upon me, because the Lord has anointed and commissioned me to bring good news to the humble and afflicted; He has sent me to bind up the wounds of the brokenhearted, to proclaim release [from confinement and condemnation] to the physical and spiritual captives and freedom to prisoners, to proclaim the favorable year of the Lord, and the day of vengeance and retribution of our God, to comfort all who mourn, to grant to those who mourn in Zion the following: to give them a turban instead of dust on their heads, a sign of mourning, the oil of joy instead of mourning, the garment expressive of praise instead of a disheartened spirit. so they will be called the trees of righteousness strong and magnificent, distinguished for integrity, justice, and right standing with God, the planting of the Lord, that He may be glorified."* This is the work of the Spirit. It was not just Jesus who came, it was Jesus and the Holy Spirit!

## THE WORK OF THE SPIRIT

When Jesus said in John 16:11 the Holy Spirit would convict the world of *judgment,* He is not bringing judgment upon *you.* He is bringing judgment upon the rulers of darkness, the principalities, the hosts of wickedness and upon Satan himself. The word judgment is connected to the word vengeance. The greatest misconception a Christian can make is to assume that the Father is angry at you. This is the ultimate deception that keeps a Christian from executing the power of the gift of Christ. When Jesus went to the cross and defeated sin through the shedding of His blood, He did, once and for all, settle the wages of sin (Hebrews 9:11-14) meaning that your sin was paid for in full and you are now exonerated, (liberated) no longer imprisoned or limited, meaning you have been granted full access to the benefits (favor) offered to sons and daughters of God.

Notice the scripture I referenced in Hebrews 9 indicates that the blood of Jesus cleanses the conscience representing that you can fully receive all that Jesus accomplished and you can think and expect as an *overcomer*. Not as one who expects condemnation, but as one who not only receives life, but victorious life. This turns the tables on the enemy. The hunted becomes the hunter! Jesus became sin on the cross so that you could live victoriously with your attention focused on the voice of the Holy Spirit instead of the condemning voice of the demonic powers of the earth.

Make no mistake about it, you have enemies! *1 Peter 5:8 says, "Satan goes about like a roaring lion seeking whom he may devour."* The second greatest deception is that you do not have spiritual enemies! Satan works to stay hidden behind the scenes, but in my experience, demonic powers are actually at the heart of the biggest problems in people's lives. In many cases, demonic powers are behind sickness, depression, anxiety, fear and many other so-called human problems (Luke 13:11). In many crusades throughout India and deliverance ministry in the USA, I have seen deaf mutes healed instantly, people with continuous flows of blood for years healed instantly, people accused of being out of their minds and experiencing rage, healed instantly when demons are driven away.

When I interview these people after deliverance, they say

things like *I was normal until that night when I was fourteen and an evil presence came into my room and from that time forward I was mute...(or deaf or had a disease, or many other limitations.)* After seeing this pattern, I have grown to not just realize the degree to which we fight the devil and his dark forces but have grown to hate the ease with which he ravages the defenseless people of the world. I have grown to understand what Jesus meant when He said, *My Father's vengeance is in My heart (Isaiah 63:4),* because His mission is to destroy the evil work of Satan (1 John 3:8) and establish people clothed in the power of the Holy Spirit who will walk in the full authority of Christ, executing the supernatural power the Lord commanded us to execute.

*Mark 16:17-18 "And these signs will follow those who believe: In My name they will cast out demons; they will speak with new tongues; 18 they will take up serpents; and if they drink anything deadly, it will by no means hurt them; they will lay hands on the sick, and they will recover."* The world is in dire need for the sons of God to be revealed in the fullness of all three Davidic promises of the Holy Spirit, especially the vengeance of our God.

The work of the Spirit of God was prophesied in *Isaiah 10:27,* *"It shall come to pass in that day that his burden will be taken away from your shoulder, and his yoke from your neck, and the yoke will be destroyed because of the anointing oil."* This is a work of the Spirit of God sent to deliver you out of the grip of darkness. The presence of the Holy Spirit breaks the yoke. Yokes of bondage include cancer, depression, pain, broken hearts, and many forms of disease and spiritual torment. It doesn't matter what form of darkness is upon your life. Jesus sent the Holy Spirit to execute judgment upon the darkness and set you free in mind, body, soul and spirit. Jesus paid it all and He sent the Holy Ghost to be an enemy of your enemies.

You are a hunter! You are a giant killer in Christ! The person who was once demonized and tormented day and night, turns the tables through the authority of Christ and begins to execute the vengeance that is embodied in the heart of Christ. The Spirit of God executes this judgment on Satan and the dark forces of this earth. See these scriptures for a further understanding of the *dunamis* power of the Holy Spirit to execute vengeance against *your* enemies, which become *the enemies of God* (see Isaiah 63:4, Isaiah 35:4, Isaiah 61:2, Psalm 58:10-11, and Exodus 23:20-33).

When you receive the Holy Spirit, your embrace and expectation of the Spirit of God to execute the rightful judgments of God against your enemies is crucial for your own personal deliverance as well as for you to step into being who the Lord says you are. Don't be deceived. Just as Satan came to Adam and deceived him from being a son of God with access to all power, Satan whispers in our ears and works to establish false identities, but the Holy Spirit is your *avenger* and will bring deliverance into your life.

The power of believing must be centered in recognition of the accomplishment of the cross. When Jesus went to the cross, the Bible says in 2 Corinthians 5:21 *"For He made Him who knew no sin to be sin for us, that we might become the righteousness of God in Him."*

Jesus was led to the cross to take the curse of sin to the cross (Galatians 3:13). So, when He (the curse) died on the cross, the curse was broken. Jesus did what no man could do. Jesus did what the Law of Moses could not do, fulfilling the desire of God to cover man in the blood of Jesus (the true living sacrifice), so now God looks at all believers through the lens of the blood, seeing all believers as clean and righteous. This is one of the greatest weapons in warfare. Knowing that God Himself is for you and not against you, not condemning you for your acts of sin, but liberating you to fullness through the resurrection.

As Christ was resurrected by the Holy Spirit, the baptism (complete immersion) into the Holy Spirit produces resurrection in your life. That is why Jesus sent the Spirit. Again, Jesus conquered sin so that you can live in the presence of the Holy Spirit hearing His voice and conquering every enemy that comes against you. You are the righteousness of God in Christ. But only the Spirit of God resurrects sons and daughters to their rightful positions as heir and joint heir in Christ (Romans 8:14-17). True adoption happens as a work of the Holy Spirit.

The mindset of righteousness is necessary to live victoriously in Christ and discern the voice of your enemy because Satan's only strategy is to deceive you from what you have been given in Christ. *2 Corinthians 10:3-6 "For though we walk in the flesh, we do not war according to the flesh. For the weapons of our warfare are not carnal but mighty in God for pulling down strongholds, casting down arguments and every high thing that exalts itself against the knowledge of God, bringing every thought into captivity to the obedience of Christ, and being ready to punish all disobedience when your obedience is fulfilled."*

From the thought process of knowing you are the beloved, like David who always ran back to the presence of God and was able to hear His voice, we all are called through Christ, the Son of David, to be of this same mindset, running into the arms of God day after day knowing we are loved. We must be ready at all times to break through feelings of depression, brokenness, demonic torment and the diseases the enemy sends our way. Running day after day into the presence of God, depending upon the Holy Spirit to resurrect us day after day, this is the lifestyle that David and Jesus demonstrated. They made the enemy was their footstool. They lived victoriously. They lived as sons truly adopted into the baptism of the Holy Spirit. They ruled (as kings) from a place of being positioned in the presence of God. This position is the throne promised to those who set their hearts on the Holy Spirit. The Spirit of God releases the favor He promised to bestow on sons and daughters of God. You are the salt of the earth (Mathew 5:13).

## SPIRITUAL IMPARTATION

My experience with the Holy Spirit is that He will do things that are beyond your expectations and even beyond your wildest imagination! When you begin to truly work with the Holy Spirit, you will quickly realize that His design is to reveal Jesus Christ and His method is through supernatural power (John 3:27; 1 Corinthians 1:1-5). The authority of Christ is manifest in judging righteously which always has a design of deliverance, setting the captives free, healing the broken hearted, opening the prison doors and bringing site to the blind. This authority manifests through promise and is a work of the Spirit.

The Spirit of God is seeking partners, co-laborers, ambassadors and most importantly adopted sons and daughters who know they are loved, to introduce the world to the love of the Holy Spirit, God's very presence on earth. The Apostle Paul is illustrated as a model ambassador of the kingdom of heaven having written most of the books in the new covenant. He walked in the power of the Spirit having signs, wonders and miracles happen everywhere He went.

He had a heart that burned, seeking to introduce all to the living God. *Paul's mission was not to introduce people to a written*

*Bible, but to introduce people to the living God.* He said in *Romans 1:11, "For I long to see you, that I may impart to you some spiritual gift, so that you may be established."* The word *impart* is the Greek word **metadidomi** meaning *to share uniquely by introduction, the introduction of a person.*

Paul was saying that he was not just coming to awaken spiritual gifts, but to introduce the Romans to the person of the Holy Spirit, the One Christ died for so that the world could be introduced to the living God, the Holy Spirit. Not just words on paper, but the tangible presence of God Himself. The very presence of the kingdom of God on earth. The One King David knew so intimately. Why? Because the Holy Spirit, the supernatural person that Jesus sent would establish you, grounding you at Zion and rebuilding the tent of David in your life. It will be the dwelling of God where sickness, disease, torment and every form of the curse of sin would be driven away. This is why Paul went on the missions he was sent to go on by the Spirit. He didn't go just to preach the written words. He went to introduce the world to the One Jesus sent called the Holy Spirit.

Ambassadors of Christ, or *co-laborers* as the Bible calls them, (true preachers), introduce the Holy Spirit to a dying world and the Spirit resurrects those bound in death and sin. This is the job of a *sent one,* offering the *safe place* of the Salt Covenant to the world.

*2 Corinthians 2:1-4, "And I, brethren, when I came to you, did not come with excellence of speech or of wisdom declaring to you the testimony of God. For I determined not to know anything among you except Jesus Christ and Him crucified. I was with you in weakness, in fear, and in much trembling. And my speech and my preaching were not with persuasive words of human wisdom, but in demonstration of the Spirit and of power, that your faith should not be in the wisdom of men but in the power of God."*

## THE RESURRECTION POWER OF THE SPIRIT

In 2017 I was in a city on the east coast of India. I was preaching in front of several thousand people and on the way to the crusade, the Lord changed everything I was planning to do. The new mission was simple. He gave me a vision of people walking into a new School of Prophecy that would be built in this city. I saw hundreds of people coming and when they walked into the room, I was standing with the Holy Spirit and introducing the Holy Spirit to every person who came through the door.

When they would reach out their hand to shake the hand of the Holy Spirit, they would fall to the ground. While they were on the ground, they were undressed by angels and new, kingly clothes would be placed upon the people. When they stood up, they would reach for the Holy Spirit and together they would walk out into the streets and they would do the same thing I was doing. They would introduce people on the street to the Holy Spirit and in turn the same thing would happen to them. I then heard the Lord say, *Tonight I (Holy Spirit) am being introduced to the people!*

When I arrived at the crusade, I did not preach as in a normal crusade type approach. I simply gave the vision of the Lord and had the people come forward. I started laying hands on the people. There was a young man in the front row who had been carried forward by several men, while an old man stood with them. They all pointed to the young man that they held by the arms as he struggled to break their grip. I laid my hand on the young man's head and he flew backwards about ten feet breaking out of the grip of those holding him. Everybody stood in shock. After about 30 seconds, the boy sat up and looked at the old man and started to talk. The old man fell to his knees with his hands in the air, crying so hard that he wailed in front of the whole crowd. The boy kept talking and those holding him were in shock.

I turned to my interpreter seeking understanding of what happen. A few minutes went by and the interpreter said that this family worships idols and five years ago, when this boy was 14, he went to bed a normal young man and able to talk. When he woke up the next morning the boy was mute and deaf. At night the young man would become violent, hurting himself and others so his father had to tie him to the four corners of the bed for his own safety every night for the last five years. The old man is his father and the reason he is screaming is because he says he just witnessed the miracle of Jesus Christ and today he renounces his idols and gives his life and the life of his family to Jesus Christ. The young man stood there laughing and crying and talking for the first time in five years, having previously been constrained by demonic powers through the idol worship practiced by their family. We brought them on stage and they testified. The whole crowd of two thousand people rushed to the altar and renounced their idols. They were all filled with the Holy Spirit and prayed in tongues!

The Holy Spirit had a plan that night to introduce Himself to the people. The Spirit revealed His resurrection power to the family that worshipped idols and were bound by demons. The introduction of the Spirit of God positioned this family to preach that night. They were the ones given a stage to testify immediately to 2,000 people and then see the immediate fruit of thousands baptized (immersed) in the Holy Spirit. I was always a proponent of the Holy Spirit, but this night challenged even my own expectations of the Holy Spirit. It changed my ministry from *trying to reveal the meaning of scripture,* to *introducing the Holy Spirit.* These were the actual last words of Jesus before He ascended into heaven, *you MUST wait and be introduced to the Holy Spirit and His **dunamis** power* (Acts 1:4-8, Luke 24:49).

# 3

# THE VOICE OF THE ANOINTING, SUPPLICATION AND THE GRACE OF TONGUES

## INTRODUCTION TO SPIRITUAL EQUIPPING

Zechariah 12:10 "And I will pour on the house of David and on the inhabitants of Jerusalem the Spirit of grace and supplication; then they will look on Me whom they pierced..."

DURING MY FIRST MISSION TO INDIA, I WAS AWARE THAT THINGS were going to be different, but I did not fully grasp the degree to which the Lord was going to use me to introduce people to the Holy Spirit, spiritual prayer and all of the equipping of the gifts of the Holy Spirit. In the very first crusade I did in India, we had about 1,000 people. After preaching, I asked the people to come forward to meet the Holy Spirit.

To my surprise the whole crowd came forward and when I started to pray, they started to weep and shake as the power of the Spirit came upon them. Almost in unison, the whole crowd started praying in tongues. It was like a symphony. As soon as they started praying in tongues, people started screaming with excitement. We sent ushers into the crowd to see what was happening, all the while continuing to pray in tongues. The ushers started bringing people to the stage to tell what was happening. Several blind people were suddenly able to see. Many deaf and mute people were able to hear and talk. A crippled man even walked. One woman was ecstatic as she came with a cancerous lump on her neck the size of an apple and it disappeared.

Many more personal miracles happened that night as we kept the crowd at the altar encountering the person of the Holy Spirit, the *Miracle Worker*. Praying in tongues continued for several hours. By the end of the meeting people were shaking in the presence of God. Some were standing, many were kneeling, but all were undone by the power of the Holy Spirit as they were introduced to the person of the Holy Spirit.

## THE GRACE OF BEING EQUIPPED BY THE HOLY SPIRIT

*Zechariah 12:10, And I will pour on the house of David and on the inhabitants of Jerusalem the Spirit of grace and supplication; then they will look upon Me whom they pierced...*

The Lord makes an amazing equipping promise to all of humanity. The house of David in this context is his heart and soul, while the inhabitants of Jerusalem represent those who followed David to Zion and became part of the outpouring of the Holy Spirit. All of this happened in a time when the Law of Moses ruled and the Holy Spirit came to only a very select few. The great anointing was passed through David's heart, who carried the Holy Spirit in a time when that just did not happen. Even more amazing is that those who stood with David, became men of renown. They were mighty men, who also killed giants, performed incredible feats, but more importantly sought the presence of the Lord (2 Samuel 23).

The Lord promised to pour out the Spirit of grace and supplication. Obviously, more than we even realize, the gift of supernatural prayer, the supplication of the Spirit, is a supernatural key that changes the game. Everything on earth is subject to the voice of God (Hebrews 1:3), therefore when He places such a high value on equipping believers with the ability to pray supernaturally with tongues, it is for the reason that it will produce *supernatural results*. Supplication is the gifting that was upon David to seek the Lord in a special and unique form of prayer. Supplication (Greek word *deomai*) means *to petition -and beseech the Lord until becoming one with Him, aligned in Spirit, envisioned by His voice.*

It is a gift equipping a person to expect in the Father's response to such a degree that a person cries out and petitions Him till He comes and speaks, meaning the supernatural ability to pray will even draw the Father to speak out of heaven. This supplication induces the promise of grace to a person's life. Grace in the new covenant is the Greek word **Charis**. *John 1:16-17, "And of His fullness we have all received, and grace for grace. For the Law was given through Moses, but grace and truth came through Jesus Christ."* So, grace is a gift through Christ, which is not possible by man working to achieve the Law of Moses or even appear righteous by doing good. Grace can only be received as a gift. This amazing gift of grace is the equipping power and blessing that Jesus Christ bestows upon sons and daughters.

The actual meaning of **grace for grace**, is the Greek phrase **grace-anti-grace** meaning *wave after wave of grace.* Once you learn to receive it, there is always the expectation of more grace coming because that is what Jesus Christ does. He sends wave after wave of grace (equipping). The gift of tongues equips a person to receive grace after grace, like what happened to the people in India who prayed in tongues for the first time. I did not pray for a single person to get healed or delivered. I prayed for them to be introduced to the Holy Spirit (baptized in the Holy Spirit) and the Spirit of God equipped them with the gift of tongues. In turn when they prayed in tongues, in supplication to the Lord, supernatural healing and deliverance began to break out, impacting the entire crowd. Tongues equipped the crowd as a gate of heaven releasing the power of the presence of the Spirit to the people. Praying in tongues produces miracles, signs and wonders.

## YOUR PERSONAL CALL TO PRAY SUPERNATURALLY

The key however to receiving grace is to join your heart with His heart. The gift of tongues is the key that makes this connection. This is where you turn your gaze to the Spirit of God and give Him your time and desire through prayer and supplication. Paul implores believers to pray in this manner in *Ephesians 6:18, pray always with all prayer and supplication in the Spirit...*

Supplication is a gifting which turns your heart to expect *the Lord Himself* in all things. Many people claim faith, but when things get tough and do not go their way, they don't turn to the Holy Spirit and wait upon Him, instead they turn to the world to pacify their current situation. The church in this hour needs great supplication. Put it this way, each of the eleven remaining disciples left the side of Jesus on the night of the crucifixion, but after they received the Holy Spirit on the day of Pentecost, all of them were faithful unto death! They were equipped with something that gave them a strength and ability in impossible situations, to stay steadfast and overcome. All eleven disciples were faithful unto death after the Holy Spirit came upon them. The only way in which this happens is through the special equipping of the Holy Spirit! A people who become Spirit dependent through this equipping of the Spirit will do supernatural things.

The pattern that Jesus demonstrated after being baptized in the Holy Spirit, was to be alone with the Spirit, in supplication with expectation of an equipping for the next mission or the issues of the day (see Matt 26:36, Luke 6:12, Matt 14:23, Mark 6:46). This dependence and expectation in prayer and supplication was a way of life for Christ. Not only was He baptized in the Holy Spirit, but His daily life was built upon utter dependence and expectation of the work of the Spirit. The *Dunamis* power of the Spirit manifested in the life of Jesus everywhere He went. He drew upon the power of the Spirit.

Many believers and even entire denominations rationalize why the Holy Spirit and the gift of tongues is not needed. However, the pattern of the outpouring of the Holy Spirit included the supernatural equipping of the voice of the anointing, the language of heaven. The pattern in the outpouring of the Spirit is always documented with tongues, followed by prophecy. We will discuss prophecy in an upcoming chapter. First, we will focus on the equipping of tongues and why it is so important in the life of every believer.

## INDUCING *YOUR* ADVOCATE

What if I told you that when you received the Holy Spirit, you received the judge and jury that was sent to ensure your deliverance to the fullness of the Father's promise. It only requires prayer and supplication to activate the Advocate. Romans 8:26-27 reveals a very deep understanding to what is actually happening when a person prays in tongues, the very endowment of supplication promised to those who become the house of God (sons of David).

Before we jump into this scripture, it is important to understand that Jesus spent three full chapters in John 14, 15 and 16 talking about the coming of the Holy Spirit and what the Holy Spirit would do when He came. Jesus called Him by the Greek name *Parakletos* meaning *the One who advocates in your favor and executes judgment against your enemy in your favor.* It means One who is called to your side before a judge, to aid in counsel and defense, and to intercede and stand in the gap between you and death ensuring your deliverance. Wow!! Now you know why Jesus was so adamant after He rose from the grave and before He ascended into heaven when He said *DO NOT LEAVE THIS CITY UNTIL I SEND **PARAKLETOS**, The Spirit of Truth who will lead you into all truth (Luke 24:49, John 14:15-18, John 16:7-15).*

We must learn how to INDUCE our advocate, our *Parakletos!* Most Christian don't know they have an Advocate or how to pray and induce the work of the Advocate. The Advocate is not optional, He is necessary. Overcoming is a work of the Spirit. *Romans 8:26-27 AMP So too the Holy Spirit (Parakletos) comes to our aid and bears us up in our weakness; for we do not know what prayer to offer nor how to offer it worthily as we ought, but the Spirit Himself goes to meet our supplication and pleads on our behalf with unspeakable yearnings and groanings too deep for utterance. And He Who searches the hearts of men knows what is in the mind of the Holy Spirit, because the Spirit intercedes (raises up a standard) and pleads before God on behalf of the saints according to and in harmony with God's will.* So, according to verse 26, somehow Jesus makes this a fool-proof process that can only be accessed by faith. You see, only by faith can one pray in tongues because tongues is the pure language of heaven (Zephaniah 3:9) and it comes only out of the reborn spirit of sons and daughters of God. It is the language that Jesus understands in heaven.

Jesus gave this pure prayer language to bypass the limitations of the souls of men and women. Through the miracle resurrection power of the Holy Spirit, the spirit of reborn sons and daughters can pray in a supernatural language that induces *Parakletos* to advocate for us in our weakness. Not only that, this supernatural language is the voice of the Spirit vocalizing the perfect will of God. This language is perfect in that it induces *Parakletos* to advocate in your favor expressing the perfect will of the Father who is for you and not against you. And, every time the enemy comes at you, Satan is destined for defeat because of *Parakletos*.

This understanding gives you insight as to why Paul was such a proponent of praying in tongues. There is no way I would be prepared to go to India and see the supernatural miracles, signs and wonders that I have seen including thousands upon thousands of people being baptized in the Holy Spirit and praying in tongues, if I did not rely, trust and expect, in *Parakletos*! The gift of tongues is key to this relationship.

## THE NATURE OF *PARAKLETOS*

There is a prophecy in Isaiah 59 that illustrates the very nature of Parakletos. *Isaiah 59:19, When the enemy comes in like a flood, The Spirit of the Lord will lift up a standard against him.* This promise goes hand-in-hand with the promise of the Father in Luke 24:49 and what was explained in such detail in John 14, 15 and 16 with the coming promise of the Holy Spirit. Jesus vows in this prophecy that when the enemy comes in like a flood, the Spirit (*Parakletos*) would raise up a standard against it, bringing judgment against your enemy. The very judgment promised in Genesis 3:15 decreeing the crushing of the head of Satan and his army.

The term *flood* is symbolic of something that appears overwhelming, but the term *standard* in Hebrew means to *drive away, overtake, conquer, put the enemy to flight.* If you connect this understanding with the fact that Jesus prophesied saying, *Out of your belly will flow living water,* your supernatural prayer language is a deluge (an overwhelming flow of the Holy Spirit) that is bigger than any flood the enemy can muster and when you pray in the Holy Ghost, you invite *Parakletos* to the party.

When *Parakletos* is invited to the party, you can't lose because the whole thing is rigged in your favor. You may have nights of challenge and disappointment and impossible odds, but supplication through the gift of tongues induces victory through the Advocate sent to judge in your favor. You must engage every battle supernaturally. Your strength is spiritual, empowered by the Holy Spirit. Supplication and tongues is the activation of *Parakletos* power who stands for you and against the darkness that accuses you day and night.

## THE TONGUES OF PRISONERS

The Holy Spirit challenged me to pray in tongues six hours every day for one year. Initially I did not know why or for what reason, but in simple obedience, I started praying. Several months into this supernatural season of prayer, I started having visitations from Jesus who would introduce me to angels by telling me their names and what their purpose was for aiding me in what He was calling me to do.

During this season, I ministered at one of the local state prisons. While I was on my way to the prison one afternoon, I was looking at my notes for a simple salvation message. The Holy Spirit started speaking to me saying "Today we are going to introduce everybody to the gift of tongues!" Initially I was concerned because the prison chaplain was not fond of anybody who ministered using the gifts of the Spirit and several men before me were asked not to come back because of things like teaching on *tongues* and *deliverance*. After a few minutes of debate, I felt this immense peace and power come upon me. I knew what I had to do, so I arrived and went through the normal process to get into the prison. The chaplain came to get me and took me to the room where there were approximately 40 prisoners.

I started to explain the Holy Spirit and then I mentioned the "T" word (tongues). I started by asking if anybody prayed in tongues. There was one man out of 40 who knew the Holy Spirit and prayed in tongues. In addition, five prisoners sitting on my right side with their backs against the wall started to heckle me. They believed doctrines which refused the Holy Spirit, especially tongues. The more I talked about the Holy Spirit and tongues, the more these guys laughed and mocked me. In addition, the chaplain was in the back of the room and I could tell he was not happy with my discussion topic, yet at the same time, there were men who were on the edge of their seat as I talked about *Parakletos* and what happened on the day of Pentecost.

After about thirty minutes the supernatural power of the Holy Spirit entered the room. One of the guys sitting beside the hecklers started weeping and the gift of tongues suddenly came out of his mouth. The whole room, including the Chaplain, looked like deer caught in the headlights as they watched and listened to this guy praying in the power of the Holy Spirit. Then, a second guy started praying in tongues. Then a third and then a fourth. Suddenly, the same men who knew nothing about the Holy Spirit before entering the room, were now praying in tongues. There were men on their knees weeping and praying. There were others who were laughing and praying.

One by one, over a period of a few minutes, the gift of tongues was imparted to these men. As all of this was going on, I turned and realized that even four out five of the hecklers sitting against the wall, were now praying in tongues. The only person not praying in tongues was the ringleader of the hecklers. He was now the only one left in the room who did not pray in tongues. He was left speechless, as the Holy Spirit confirmed the Day of Pentecost to 39 out of 40 men in the room.

I learned that day the importance of obeying the voice of the Holy Spirit above any form of rationalization. There is no substitute for the voice of God and the power that He sends with His instruction in your life. He truly does confirm His words, when He directly speaks to you, with signs and wonders (Mark 16:20). The true power of the Spirit is carried by sons and daughters who know the living God and hear His voice. The Bible alone was not the goal. The goal is that you *hear His voice!*

# 4

## THE VISION MULTIPLIES


### CAN I INTRODUCE YOU TO THE HOLY SPIRIT?

Matthew 16:18-19 "And I also say to you that you are Peter, and on this rock I will build My church, and the gates of Hades shall not prevail against it. And I will give you the keys of the kingdom of heaven, and whatever you bind on earth will be bound in heaven, and whatever you loose on earth will be loosed in heaven."

THERE WAS A PASTOR IN A SMALL VILLAGE IN INDIA WHO HAD BEEN writing to me for years asking me to come. So, I found a way to fit him into my schedule after I had been prompted by the Holy Spirit. It was different from the normal crusade work that I do. He did not have the capabilities to coordinate large crusades, but I was led to do ministry with this pastor. So, we had a pastor's conference scheduled and we were expecting about 100 pastors. On the morning of the conference, the Holy Spirit woke me up and started to speak to me about a pregnant woman who was in a fight to carry the child full term. The Lord showed me a vision of a python wrapped around the pregnant woman's belly, constricting the baby's growth, trying to abort the pregnancy and prevent it from being birthed. The Lord said, *What you see happening to this baby is a picture of the constriction that is on the church in India. This woman will give birth! Prophesy to the baby and prophesy to the church in India. Prophecy that I will pour out my Spirit in this nation!*

Within minutes of this discussion with the Holy Spirit, the pastor called me and said, *you are not going to believe this but there are already 200 pastors gathered at the meeting place.* Thirty minutes later he called and said, *there are 300 pastors gathered now*! He was panicked because we did not prepare for that many people. By the time they picked me up and I arrived at the meeting, to my amazement, 430 pastors came from areas far and wide. Many required days of travel to get to the meeting. Many were saying they had dreams from the Holy Spirit prompting them to come.

When we started the meeting, I asked if anybody knew the Holy Spirit with prophecy and praying in tongues. Only 30 pastors were baptized in the Holy Spirit. The other 400 did not know the Holy Spirit. I then asked if there was any pastor who was pregnant. One woman stood up. She was in the final month of pregnancy and the other pastors that knew her were saying that she was having complications in carrying the child. Imagine that, the very thing the Holy Spirit showed me in the vision, a woman being constricted in pregnancy. I started to laugh inside because I knew she was a single prophetic symbol of what was going to happen that day. I prophesied that *she and the church would not be constricted by the serpent, but Jesus Christ was present to uncoil the restrictions on the church and that just as this woman would give birth, so would the church in India. The Church in India would experience an outpouring of the Holy Spirit and it multiply!*

By the end of the meeting, all 430 pastors were baptized in the Holy Spirit, praying in tongues. Many miracles happened with the pastors that day, but the most important thing was the impartation of faith that occurred to these pastors because they discovered that the fight was not theirs alone in a nation that does not embrace Christianity. They received the impartation of faith and the prophecy of the Holy Spirit, because they were on the heart of the Lord and they discovered that Jesus sent a man from the other side of the world to impart the vision of victory for them and the bride of Christ in India. I found out a month later that the woman's pregnancy complications ended that very day and she gave birth to a healthy baby boy. This is a prophetic picture of the bride of Christ multiplying by the power of the Holy Spirit.

## THE VOICE AND THE SCRIPTURE

Jesus said in *Luke 9:13, Occupy till I come,* but very few truly grasp the power and authority of this command. The command is not a frivolous statement simply connecting to a person's thought that they have been given authority from Jesus (Matthew 28:18-20). The command to *go* is also connected to the command to love God. Loving God is a function of your relationship with the Holy Spirit where there is direct hearing of the voice of God (John 17:21, John 10:27-28).

I see many people in the wrong place at the wrong time doing what we would call *spiritual work* such as preaching and teaching and doing good things. This includes people who think they are pastors or evangelists to other nations but were never called to do certain things. Vision is key. Without vision and the spiritual impartation that sends people for a specific work, much of what the body of Christ does is dead works producing little or no fruit. Fruit is a product of multiplication and the vision the Lord speaks is the only thing capable in the Kingdom of producing and multiplying fruit. Any work, including spiritual work, that is not generated through the voice of God sending people, ends up being chaff and stubble in the wind. There is no substitute for the voice of the Spirit. It is central to the relationship that Jesus desires with all sons and daughters of God. It is extremely important that we know that authority is connected to purpose, and *purpose always has a time and place for execution.*

The Holy Spirit asked me a question a long time ago: *Can the Bible be philosophy?* At first, I questioned who or what was questioning me because I grew up thinking that the Bible alone was God. Before you get all bent out of shape, let me clarify. I grew up in a denomination that believes the Bible is the Word of God. I believe with all my heart that the Holy Bible is breathed by God. It documents what God spoke over the generations and the acts of those who believed Him, as well as the prophecies of things to come and the Law of Moses. However, God reigns in heaven with Christ at His right hand and the Holy Spirit on earth. They are bigger than what they provided you on paper.

So when the question was posed by the Holy Spirit, I was initially confused. My initial response was *"no" it cannot be philosophy.* However, the Holy Spirit started asking me questions and led me down a path of understanding to clarify between the Bible interpreted by the Holy Spirit versus the Bible interpreted through a false motive of man, as well as the spirit of this age (Satan). The Bible clearly states that even the demons believe the scripture, but that does not make them holy. It actually supports the fact that they purposefully choose to rebel and intended to deceive like their father the devil. Therefore, these spirits can do great damage to people who read the scripture but are deceived in their motivation by twisting what is true, making people believe in a *system* rather than the intent of knowing the living God. The Bible is meant to be an introduction to the ways of God. It is a love letter, so to speak, that reveals the intention for you *to know God in spirit and in truth* (John 4:24).

## BLINDED BY THE SCRIPTURE WITHOUT THE SPIRIT

Jesus functioned under the leading of the Spirit which was a vast contrast with the Pharisees and Sadducees who followed the Bible as a rule book. Jesus received fresh words (visions and dreams) revealing the place where He was going next, what His mission was, and who His audience would be each day. Jesus was always in the right place, at the right time, with the right message and mission. Each and every day of His life, as we discussed in the previous chapter, Jesus sought the Spirit to speak so that He could hear, listen and execute the command of the Spirit's voice.

In contrast, the Pharisees and Sadducees were bound to the old covenant, and even more detrimental, they made an idol out of the old covenant claiming to be righteous because they not only *followed the rules of God*, but in their self-righteous zeal, they added to it and burdened the people with *unnecessary requirements*. When Jesus came, He treated people in two different categories. To the sinners who needed a savior, He ate with them in their houses and everywhere throughout the land, but to the Pharisees and Sadducees, Jesus was consistently infuriated.

Jesus was constantly confronting the Pharisees and Sadducees calling them dead sepulchers, blind guides, whitewashed tombs and even declaring that they were *of their father the devil* (*Matthew 23, John 8:44*).

To become a Pharisee or a Sadducee, each candidate was required to memorize the first five books of the Torah (Genesis, Exodus, Leviticus, Numbers and Deuteronomy). But Jesus said something that makes a clear distinction between worshipping what is written in a philosophic manner, verses following the living voice of the Holy Spirit and *knowing God*. In *John 5:37-40 Jesus says, And the Father Himself, who sent Me, has testified of Me. You have neither heard His voice at any time, nor seen His form. But you do not have His word abiding in you, because whom He sent, Him you do not believe. You search the Scriptures, for in them you think you have eternal life; and these are they which testify of Me. But you are not willing to come to Me that you may have life.*

Jesus distinguished Himself as living by the Spirit, yet knowing what the Law says. Jesus did not tout the Law as rules. He did not carry a Bible. Jesus carried the Holy Spirit and it distinguished Him so vastly from the men that memorized the Bible (Torah) that they could not recognize Him since they were blinded by another spirit, the spirit of the age. Take note, the issue Jesus had was not that the Bible (Torah) is wrong. The Torah (Law of Moses), was written by the Finger of God. However, remember this, the words on stone (Ten Commandments) were not the original plan of God. In Exodus 20, Moses was sent down the mountain to invite the nation to see God's face just as Moses had experienced.

God wanted face-to-face relationships with His people, not just *one representative*. However, they refused the invitation, so God put words on stone and gave them rituals that could never cleanse the conscience or break the power of sin (Hebrews 9:11-15). The words on stone (now on paper) were under the subjection of the heart of man. The degree of error the Pharisees and Sadducees functioned in by the time Jesus arrived on the scene, was something that was so far away from the original design that it infuriated Jesus Christ. They made the Bible a misrepresentation of God. They made it *philosophy*.

The Pharisees and Sadducees paraded themselves around like they were better than everybody else and somehow, they were more holy in their own minds because of the rituals they subjected themselves to promoting themselves as achieving the scriptures they memorized, all the while not knowing God Himself. They were *fake* and that infuriated Jesus. The Pharisees and Sadducees bypassed the intent of the Law of Moses which was to reveal the need of a living savior, a Messiah who could fulfill the Law and bring the nations to meet the living God face-to-face. This was the original plan. It was never to put words on stone (or paper)! The original invitation was to speak face-to-face and have God write His words on the hearts of sons and daughters (Ezekiel 36:26, Hebrews 8:7-13).

Jesus was absolutely infuriated with the Pharisees and Sadducees because they made a god out of the system using what God actually spoke in years past. This actually enslaved the people instead of liberating the people. They made a system instead of a relationship. This is the exact opposite of the original invitation to the mountain of God and what Jesus came to bring in the new covenant. Notice in the four gospels that the thing Jesus fought was not sin itself, but the self-defined religious system which misrepresented God and the Holy Spirit. It ultimately was not the Romans who desired Jesus be put to death, it originated from the religious system that appeared to be holy but whose intent was to remain the centerpiece of what the people worshiped. They worshipped the system and not God. They did not even know God. If you understand this, then the intent of *why Jesus came* was not just to conquer sin but to establish a new covenant where the centerpiece was not a system, but a personal relationship (face-to-face) with the Holy Spirit, birthing in the heart of man the desire to cry out, ***show me your glory!***

Jesus came as the Son of David carrying the promise of the restoration of God dwelling with man in Spirit. Remember, the Law of Moses and its rituals with all of the *so called religious men* of the day dwelling in a building, driving people to conform to the system, while David dwelled under the shadow of the wing of the Ark in the presence of God. The spirit of prophecy flowed out of David in this place allowing men to hear the voice of God directly. The psalms and prophecies flowed to the masses in Zion in a time where it promoted continual worship twenty-four hours per day, seven days per week. This is what Jesus came to restore. Mighty men, giant killers, men who did supernatural feats like David, were created in this atmosphere by the living voice of God who creates. This power of prophetic release is the intent of Christ's design, establishing a church of power (hearing God), not conformity to a system.

## THE RESTORATION OF THE TENT OF DAVID

This is why Jesus was so adamant to get to the cross and even said He was not finished with His work when He took the keys of death and rose out of the grave with all keys of authority (Revelation 1:18, Ephesians 4:7-9). His intention was to restore the key of David to all who believe. Jesus instructed the believers to wait in Jerusalem until the power of the Holy Spirit (the key of David), was given (Acts 1:4-8). This power transforms the soul, restores the spirit and establishes the heart of sons and daughters of God to hear His voice. This theme is so central and is the design and intent of what Jesus came to accomplish that He actually warned all who try to do what the Pharisees and Sadducees did with the words written on stone. Jesus said in *Mark 3:28-30, "Truly I say to you, all sins shall be forgiven the sons of men, and whatever blasphemies they utter; but whoever blasphemes against the Holy Spirit never has forgiveness, but is guilty of an eternal sin*--because they were saying, *He has an unclean spirit."*

Jesus makes the priority of the new covenant the Holy Spirit and the design of the Holy Spirit being the One who speaks and communicates with sons and daughters of God  face-to-face. There is no substitute for this relationship. There is no amount of Bible  reading that can take the place of a person hearing the voice of the living God. In fact, Jesus reveals that there is a demonic spirit who twists the hearts of men, turning the words on paper (the Bible) into their own religion using scripture as bait, twisting the scriptures and making the Bible a *philosophy* rather than *the introduction to the living God.* **There is no substitute for the living voice of God.**

The Bible itself is not meant to be a substitute. The Spirit of God was sent to lead those who will follow the voice (Matthew 4:19). Jesus called the Pharisees and Sadducees serpents and broods of vipers, saying they were of their father the devil (John 8:44). There was a spirit of evil that deceived man into self-imposed religious worship without the Spirit of God. Jesus said this is blasphemy against the Holy Spirit because the Holy Spirit is to be the centerpiece who brings men to face-to-face relationship with God. *Blaspheme (blasphēméō) means to misrepresent or reverse the true intent or to defame.*

## YOU ARE THE CHRIST

In the revelation of who Jesus Christ is, the Mediator of the new covenant, He establishes the means by which this new covenant is entered through the Spirit of God. It is not possible to enter this covenant in any other way. No longer based on the rituals of the old covenant could it even be faked or misrepresented because this new covenant would bring life and it would be evident to all when a person is born again of the Spirit. Only the Spirit resurrects people from the tomb of death *(Hebrews 9:15-17)*. That is the grace granted through the Christ (the anointing of the Holy Spirit). Just as David was centered around the presence of God and the living prophetic voice that spoke in Zion through men and women who lived in the presence of His Spirit, Jesus vows the restoration of people being centered on the Spirit of God and not on the religious systems. Instead, Jesus reveals Himself to the disciples as the Christ (The Anointing), Not just Jesus the man in the flesh, but as Jesus Christ, the man clothed in the Holy Spirit who walks by the voice of the Spirit and not by memorized scripture.

Jesus established this new means of life as the centerpiece of His church in *Matthew 16:13-19, "When Jesus came into the region of Caesarea Philippi, He asked His disciples, saying, 'Who do men say that I, the Son of Man, am?' So they said, 'Some say John the Baptist, some Elijah, and others Jeremiah or one of the prophets.' He said to them, 'But who do you say that I am?' Simon Peter answered and said, 'You are the Christ, the Son of the living God.' Jesus answered and said to him, 'Blessed are you, Simon Bar-Jonah, for flesh and blood has not revealed this to you, but My Father who is in heaven. And I also say to you that you are Peter, and on this rock I will build My church, and the gates of Hades shall not prevail against it. And I will give you the keys of the kingdom of heaven, and whatever you bind on earth will be bound in heaven, and whatever you loose on earth will be loosed in heaven."'*

Jesus declares that He alone builds His church by speaking directly to His sons and daughters. It is in the voice of the Spirit where creation happens. Nothing is created without the fresh, direct prophetic words of Christ. The world becomes subject of the prophetic voice of Christ because the prophetic words of the Spirit actually hold death and darkness captive. Prophecy creates in the same manner in which the Lord created in Genesis 1:1-3. Nothing can be created or destroyed without first going through Christ (the anointing). The word Christ means *the anointing.* It is the Greek word **Christos** meaning **the one clothed in the Holy Spirit; to be smeared with oil of the Spirit of God.**

Jesus builds His church not through men memorizing the Bible and trying to look righteous and doing good. Jesus builds His church through sons and daughters of God who are baptized in the Holy Spirit, equipped to hear His voice and execute what He commands. His spoken words contain the power to bind and loose, to root out and to pull down, to destroy and to throw down, to build and to plant (Matthew 16:15-18, Jeremiah 1:9-10). The advantage of hearing the voice of the Holy Spirit is that He always positions you in the right time, in the right place, with the right words (vision). The disadvantage of the way of the Pharisees is that they used the written scriptures but they were entombed in death as Jesus literally called them whitewashed tombs (appearing righteous but inside there was no resurrected life since that only comes through the Holy Spirit).

They made an idol out of the true scriptures and manipulated the people through the twisting of the Bible. Consequently they were never in the right place, at the right time, with the right message. They just produced more conditions for the people to achieve, taking advantage of the people who actually believed the Bible was true. The difference between Jesus and the self-righteous leaders of the Synagogue was that Jesus introduced the world to the person of the Holy Spirit. Signs, wonders and miracles are the work of the Spirit.

The Pharisees couldn't do that because they did not know Him, and they could not even recognize Him (John 5:37-40). The Pharisees imprisoned people with twisted biblical conditions having enough truth woven in to deceive the people, but Jesus multiplied through the liberating power of the Spirit through dreams, visions and prophecy (John 5:19).

Once you understand this concept and that the intent is to hear Him speak so that He can create *in you and through you,* you become like David and center your life around the Spirit and not around the rituals of the letter of scripture. *John 1:1-5, In the beginning was the Word, and the Word was with God, and the Word was God. He was in the beginning with God. All things were made through Him, and without Him nothing was made that was made. In Him was life, and the life was the light of men. 5 And the light shines in the darkness, and the darkness did not comprehend it.*"

The intent of the use of the word "Word" in this context is not in reference to words on paper (or stone) documenting what God spoke in times past, but creation is revealed as a face-to-face relationship where the Word, the person of Christ, speaks. Jesus Christ is known in heaven as the Word of God. The Word of God is living and not simply words on paper (Revelation 19:11-15). This is the power of the prophetic voice.

Don't get me wrong, there is great value in understanding the scriptures and I believe the Holy Spirit speaks through the scriptures still today, but a major point of the power of the original design of the church is missing from a large portion of the body who relegates the Holy Spirit as an option (take it or leave it type of option), when the intent of Jesus was to re-center the church around the Spirit so sons and daughters would directly hear from Him and shake the earth through the Spirit of Prophecy (we get into this in later chapters.)

The early church did not carry a Bible. They didn't even have written scriptures. They carried the Holy Spirit and power! Their major fight was against the Gnostics who tried to make Christianity about simple knowledge of scripture. It was the same fight Jesus had with the Pharisees and Sadducees who made a god out of scripture instead of seeking to know the living God of the Bible.

## DEMONSTRATING THE WAY OF THE HOLY SPIRIT

Jesus demonstrated this life continually through the four gospels as He would *go away to pray.* Every day was a new spiritual encounter releasing heaven on earth. Jesus would go into prayer and come out leading His team to a single woman at a well, to a man chained to the tombs, to a blind man and even to feed the five thousand. His life was led by the Spirit. There is no such thing as chance. Jesus did not believe in chance or let even one day go by without going where the Spirit of God led Him.

Jesus revealed this secret way of life when He was in hot debate with the Pharisees and Sadducees as their hatred for

Jesus grew to an immense level that was the tipping point in their determination to crucify Him. *John 5:19-20, "Then Jesus answered and said to them, 'Most assuredly, I say to you, the Son can do nothing of Himself, but what He sees the Father do; for whatever He does, the Son also does in like manner. For the Father loves the Son, and shows Him all things that He Himself does; and He will show Him greater works than these, that you may marvel.'"*

The prophetic relationship through prayer is the way Jesus centered His life. He saw His Father face-to-face in prayer and it infuriated the religious leaders of the Synagogue who knew the Bible (Torah). It exposed them as *fake* as Jesus was led by the Spirit and executed what He saw in (dreams and visions) in the Spirit (John 1:48). The signs and wonders that followed Jesus were a confirmation of the communication with the Spirit of God and then when He acted on those visions and dreams, heaven was released on earth with signs, wonders and miracles.

When you grasp this spiritual concept that is centered on the Holy Spirit leading sons and daughters through life, the Lord's prayer suddenly becomes a seeking and executing process through the relationship with the Holy Spirit instead of just a regurgitated scripture.

*Matthew 6:9-10, "Our Father in heaven, hallowed be Your name. Your kingdom come. Your will be done on earth as it is in heaven."*

Jesus is revealing the means by which He was led on earth by the Spirit of God and now leading you to seek the voice of the Father and to hear His voice. This is the central theme of Spirit living in the new covenant (the restoration of the Davidic Covenant by the One who holds the keys of David) knowing that any person who hears the voice of God releases the power of heaven on earth. This is how heaven invades earth.

## WHO ARE THE REAL PREACHERS?

The Spirit of God heralds the distinction between a person who is sent by the Lord, verses a self-proclaimed religious man. *Romans 10:14-17, "How then will they call on him in whom they have not believed? And how are they to believe in him of whom they have never heard? And how are they to hear without a preacher? And how are they to preach unless they are sent? As it is written, 'How beautiful are the feet of those who preach the good news!' But they have not all obeyed the gospel. For Isaiah says, Lord, who has believed what he has heard from us? So faith comes from hearing, and hearing through the word (Rhema) of Christ."*

A true *preacher* is not just one who can read the Bible or even reference it, but a true preacher is one who hears in the Spirit like Jesus did, having dreams, visions and prophecy as their central means of going and ministering in the right time, in the right place, with the right message for the right person. In verse 14, the Greek word for preacher is "***Kerusso***," meaning "*a herald of divine truth: not just one who pronounces the Bible to congregations, but one who hears the direct voice of the Spirit which is specific to a vision or a message for a specific people in a specific time.*" The Greek word for "Word" in verse 17 is the word ***Rhema*** meaning a dream or vision or encounter where the Spirit of God reveals a message and sends that person to preach it.

This is a very distinct understanding indicating that faith is only possible to be imparted from the Lord Jesus Christ. Faith is not something mankind can create on their own, like the Pharisees who read the Bible and *faked it* by making it a system. That's what a fake preacher does. They use the Bible as a philosophical tool making it sound good, tickling the ears, but its intent is control and deception. People who only read the Bible to congregations are not *sent ones* from God.

A true *sent one* from God is one who hears the voice of God in dreams, vision and encounters with the Holy Spirit and through these impartations of faith, they take a *living message* to the people which produces life and deliverance. This is the foundation for us moving into the next section of this book where we will dive into the heart of the vision Jesus has for sons and daughters to have unlimited access to heaven so that heaven can be released on earth through true preachers who carry the Holy Spirit, the Key of David!

# 5

# THE PRAYER LANGUAGE HE HEARS

## THE GRACE OF HIS VOICE

1 Corinthians 14:15 (AMP) "Then what am I to do? I will pray with my spirit by the Holy Spirit that is within me, but I will also pray intelligently with my mind and understanding; I will sing with my spirit by the Holy Spirit that is within me, but I will sing intelligently with my mind and understanding also."

VISION IS SO IMPORTANT THAT THE BIBLE SAYS THAT *WITHOUT vision the people perish* (Proverbs 28:19). It begs the question; what is the key to obtaining vision?

A major issue that actually magnifies spiritual blindness is when a religious system centered on biblical principles takes precedence (or is taught) over the Spirit. Principles of the Bible are necessary as they establish belief on subject matter or revelations of the Spirit. However, Jesus made it very clear that the Holy Spirit is the centerpiece. The One who raised Christ from the dead and is sent to raise us also into life is the Holy Spirit. There is no substitute for His voice. All power comes from His voice and is the only means of multiplication in the kingdom of Heaven. Vision is the seed that produces trees.

It is important that you know the way of righteousness. Jesus accomplished victory on the cross, so all ability is granted to believers through this accomplishment (the act of taking sin to the grave). However, this is not the endpoint. You must learn the way of entering grace. The Apostle Paul, through the Holy Spirit, spends a great deal of time discussing the blinding way of dead religion focused on the Law of Moses and religious systems, in contrast to the way of righteousness. *Galatians 3:8-9, And the Scripture, foreseeing that God would justify the Gentiles by faith, preached the gospel to Abraham beforehand, saying,* **In you all the nations shall be blessed.** *So then those who are of faith are blessed with believing Abraham.*

Please take note that Paul, through the revelation of the Holy Spirit, is saying that the gospel was preached to Abraham. On a timeline, Abraham lived long before Moses and the Israelites received the Ten Commandments and the Law of Moses. This gospel was preached to Abraham through dreams and visions imparting life. *Genesis 15:1, 5-6 "After these things the Word of Yahweh came to Abram in a vision, saying:* **Do not be afraid, Abram; I am your shield, and your reward shall be very great...** *Then He brought him outside and said,* **Look now toward heaven, and count the stars if you are able to number them.** *And He said to him,* **So shall your descendants be.** *And he believed in the Lord, and* **He accounted it to him for righteousness.**"

Long before Moses even ascended the mountain where the law was given to him, God spoke to Abraham. Abraham believed what God spoke in a dream and it is called the gospel, and when he believed the direct voice of God he was counted as righteous (Galatians 3:9, Romans 4:1-4). It wasn't an altar call response that made Abraham righteous, it was following the voice of God, the vision imparted in dreams. Wow!

Did you get that? This will boggle your mind and shake the very deceptive religious doctrines from your soul. Simply put, the way of the Holy Spirit through dreams and visions to Abraham are referenced by Paul in Galatians 3 and Romans 4:1-4 as the way of righteousness contrasting the way that leads to death being the attempt to know God through the Law of Moses. And in addition to that, Jesus even reveals the significance of the true gospel being preached to Abraham when He responded to the question from the Pharisees as they argued with Him about being the Son of God and doing what the Spirit revealed to Him in visions, when Jesus answered them in *John 8:58, "Jesus said to them, 'Most assuredly, I say to you, before Abraham was, I AM.'"*

Abraham was given a promise through visions and dreams. Abraham believed the vision and it was accounted as ***righteousness***, ultimately producing the nation of Israel. Abraham believed the vision and Isaac was conceived from what was impossible by human means. Isaac believed his father's dream that was given to him by Abraham and Jacob was then visited by the Spirit, making a way for access to heaven through dreams (Genesis 28:10-17). Jacob believed and his name was changed to a nation (Israel) producing 12 sons, resulting in 12 tribes, resulting in a nation which was actually birthed when Abraham believed the very first dream.

This is an illustration of the true gospel which is revealed by the Holy Spirit in *Romans 5:20-21, Moreover the law entered that the offense might abound. But where sin abounded, grace abounded much more, that as sin reigned in death, even so grace might reign through righteousness to eternal life through Jesus Christ our Lord (The Word – the direct voice of Christ through dreams, visions and the gifts of the Spirit).*

Grace is not released without *vision*, and vision is a function of the Spirit of God speaking living words into your heart creating something in your heart that you could never do on your own. You essentially become a product of His voice, a new creation being built not with hands or by any organization or government, but by the Spirit (the voice) of the living God (2 Corinthians 5:1, Psalm 51:10).

## THE TEACHER'S WAY

Paul said, *I pray in tongues more than you all (1 Corinthians 14:18).* Paul had an extreme revelation of the true gospel. He lived in absolute dependence upon the Holy Spirit and this resulted in Paul praying in tongues a great amount of time. Paul was used by the Holy Spirit to reveal deep secrets and Paul did not hold anything back. He revealed this extreme contrast between worldly knowledge and spiritual knowledge revealed by the Holy Spirit. *In Ephesians 3:16-19, I pray that He would grant you, according to the riches of His glory, to be strengthened with might (kratos) through His Spirit in the inner man, that Christ may dwell in your hearts through faith; that you, being rooted and grounded in love, may be able to comprehend with all the saints what is the width and length and depth and height — to know the love (Agape) of Christ which passes knowledge (established doctrine); that you may be filled with all the fullness of God.*

Notice that Paul uses the word *knowledge* in two completely different contexts. The Spirit of God in this passage is making a clear distinction between where spiritual power comes from and it is not simply by memorizing scriptures. When Paul says, *to know the love of Christ,* it is the Greek word **ginosko** meaning *to personally experience through knowing the person (Holy Spirit) who imparts a spiritual equipping.* In this case it is the Spirit of God who imparts through dreams, visions and prophecies. Paul contrasted this way of life in the Spirit hearing the Spirit versus earthly wisdom sourced from man-made interpretation and *twisting* of scripture that God spoke in times past. Paul is talking about your personal relationship with the Holy Spirit being so deep that you are granted the *might* of the Spirit. The word *might* in verse 16 is the Greek word **kratos** meaning the power or **dunamis** that comes from direct spoken words (dreams, visions and prophecy). This is the *might of the Lord.* This is how the world was created and how heaven invades earth today. This is the power of the gospel of Jesus Christ!

Before the infamous day on the road to Damascus (Acts 9), Paul was called the Pharisee of Pharisees. He was the elite of the elite among the intelligentsia. However, after the encounter with Christ and then Ananias laying hands on Paul to receive the power of the Holy Spirit, the Bible says that scales fell off Paul's eyes. This is symbolic of the way of the serpent, Satan, who knew what God said, but chose to do it his way, separated from God. As Satan knew the scriptures, so did Paul, but Paul's own words after being baptized in the Holy Spirit were to claim he knew nothing but Christ, the living God (1 Corinthians 2:2)!

## SPIRITUAL KNOWLEDGE AND POWER

*1 Corinthians 14: 20-21, Brethren, do not be children in under-standing; however, in malice be babes, but in understanding be mature. In the law it is written: "With men of other tongues and other lips I will speak to this people; And yet, for all that, they will not hear Me," says the Lord."* This of course is a reference to Isaiah 28:9-12. Paul is using this as an illustration to the church revealing how God speaks to the church (also known as the gifts of the Spirit). These gifts are the fruit of a person who receives *kratos* power from the Lord through dreams, visions and prophecy as we have been illustrating as the way of Christ, His true gospel that has the power to transform a person/people from the inside out supernaturally and do something to the human soul, that no amount of study and learning can do alone. Only God can change a man's heart. Paul is using this as the backdrop to explain to the church in Corinth the connection between the gift of tongues and the Lord speaking to the body through individuals who know and hear the living voice of God.

Paul first illustrates the importance of praying in the Holy Spirit because prophecy always follows praying in tongues (Acts 2:4, 19:6). In *1 Corinthians 14:5  I wish you all spoke with tongues, but even more that you prophesied; for he who prophesies is greater than he who speaks with tongues, unless indeed he interprets, that the church may receive edification.* The goal then is to hear the Lord speak and that is connected to the supernatural prayer language. Tongues always induces prophecy and the gifts of the Spirit (the voice of God).

The secret is found in the scripture that Paul references in 1 Corinthians 14:20-21 which points to *Isaiah 28:9-12.* AMP *"To whom will He teach knowledge [grant revelation]? And whom will He make to understand the message? Those who are babies, just weaned from the milk and taken from the breasts? Is that what He thinks we are?  For it is His prophets repeating over and over: precept upon precept, precept upon precept, rule upon rule, rule upon rule; here a little, there a little. No, but the Lord will teach the rebels in a more humiliating way by men with stammering lips and another tongue will He speak to this people says Isaiah, and teach them His lessons. To these complaining Jews the Lord had said, This is the true rest the way to true comfort and happiness that you shall give to the weary, and, this is the true refreshing--yet they would not listen to His teaching."*

First, the word **teach** in verse 9 means to shoot arrows (words) from His bow (His heart). As the rider of the white horse carrying a bow and arrow (Revelation 19:11-15), Jesus shoots His words into your heart: meaning He comes out of heaven with all of heavens power and the words He speaks carry that power. True knowledge and understanding must be imparted though *Spirit to spirit contact.* As we have seen in our discussion of spiritual knowledge versus earthly wisdom, Jesus Christ is your teacher. You cannot possibly teach yourself. God even asks the question for you saying "is it His prophets repeating scripture" in verse 11.

He answers "NO!" He says I will teach you in a more humiliating way. This is probably the biggest culture shock for even the most astute believers. It is not possible for you to teach yourself. You can only be taught the kingdom of heaven through the Teacher – Jesus Christ, who is the Spirit of Prophecy who comes out of heaven riding a white horse and invades your soul, transforming it from the inside out through the creative power of dreams, visions and prophecy. This is the true Word – the gospel!

Second, you can bring this Teacher (Holy Spirit) to speak to you if you know the way of the Spirit. Verse 11 says that *"He will teach you with a stammering lip and another tongue."* The meaning of this Hebrew phrase is illustrated as a newborn baby crying out for the mother's milk. When the baby cries, the mother does not have to think about allowing the milk to flow. The milk flows when the baby cries. It is automatic. This is the analogy the Spirit of God uses to identify how tongues is the main key of the arsenal the Lord, granting you access to the heart of God, when you are baptized in the Holy Ghost. The Spirit equips the believer to cry out with a stammering lip and another tongue. Why? The Spirit helps us in our weakness when we do not know what to pray. Tongues induces conversation with the Spirit.

Simply put, praying in tongues produces the vision of the Spirit. When you receive the gift of tongues, you are now equipped, like a baby, to stop thinking as a man, and use the way of the Spirit, praying supernaturally and drawing God Himself to turn and look your way and to give you the nourishment you need including His presence, visions, dreams and prophecy. All of heaven is at the tip of your tongue.

Wow! Wow! Wow! This is why Jesus was so adamant when He said stay in this city because I am going reconnect your Spirit to the Living God (Acts 1:4-8). Jesus became the door, the gate of heaven when He took sin to the grave and ascended to heaven to send you the Holy Spirit. You now have the ability to hear the voice of God and receive *dunamis* transforming power when His *kratos* words (visions, dreams and prophecy) are released from Heaven. This is why Paul said I pray in tongues more than you all. Not only did signs, wonders and miracles follow Paul, but He sought the Lord so uniquely that wisdom and understanding was granted through spiritual prayer to explain the true meaning of the scripture. And breaking free even the Jew from the bondage of scripture, and the sinner from the bondage of the world. The new covenant grants access to the most powerful force in the universe, the heart of God through the Holy Spirit. This is the rebuilding of the tent of David (Amos 9:11) and the restoration of government established by the Son of David (Isaiah 22:22). You are the house of God! Mighty men are being awakened as the Lord is restoring supernatural prayer and supplication in this hour.

## THE LANGUAGE OF SONS

When a father and son are connected in spirit, there is a commitment and level of caring that is beyond explanation. In this care and commitment, the son learns the father's language, not vice-versa. King David and the Father were committed to each other far beyond anything that happened in the temple of worship. Every place David went, the Father was with Him and actually went before him to establish his victory before David stepped foot on the battlefield. There was a desperate supplication that came out of David, praying diligently to the Father and the Father always spoke in a language that David understood. David demonstrated supplication in the Spirit expecting His Father to hear him and then answer him. This is the pattern of the Spirit, you pray His language, He answers you, you prophesy the vision and execute (Acts 2:4, 19:6! Without a desperate heart to hear the Father, the son walks blind.

King David demonstrated expectation in the Spirit continually through supplication and obedience to His Father's voice, knowing that His voice contained all power to create, dictate and establish David in the situation that was before him. David's love for the presence of God and expectation of the Lord's continual deliverance made a way for God to continually create victory in David's life. As an example, when David was made king, the Philistines immediately rallied to fight against him and challenge his new kingship. They did this twice within the first year of his reign as king, each time going to meet David and his army in the Valley of Rephaim, also known as the Valley of Giants (2 Samuel 5:17-25).

Prior to the first battle, David sought direction from the Lord. The Lord responded with instructions to go directly into the valley. David then acted as instructed and the Philistines were defeated. Soon after, the Philistines rallied again and went to meet David in the same valley. David then portrayed his absolute dependence on the Holy Spirit. Instead of thinking in a routine fashion, David stopped and prayed to the Father for direction. David could have said that the Lord already spoke the first time and David could have just led his army directly into battle. However, David did not bypass seeking the Lord, he realized the Lord could do a new thing. The Bible says that when David sought the Lord prior to the second battle, the Lord told him to wait adjacent to the mulberry trees, saying *"When you hear the marching sound of the angels in trees, then advance onto the battlefield."*

David did exactly as the Lord instructed and when he went out to battle the second time, it was essentially over before he stepped foot on the battlefield. The angel of the Lord and His army were heard in the wind going through the trees and the Philistines were defeated supernaturally. The Lord demonstrated providing two different paths of action, at two different times, from the same place. Although the battle happened at the same place with the same enemy, David's supplication to the Lord revealed a new strategy each time. What is we expected in God to truly do a new thing, even from the same place? The lesson here is absolute Holy Spirit dependence. David demonstrated how to wait and expect in God for the new thing of the Holy Spirit in a manner that is completely different from dead religious doctrines which imprison people to do the same thing in the same place according to their own false expectations. We need *Davids* who are absolutely dependent upon the Holy Spirit to do a different supernatural thing every day of their lives even if they remain in the same place battling the same thing. David's strength was that he expected God in everything and assumed nothing based on previous experiences!

## PROPHESY THE DREAM!

To illustrate this concept, I want to share an experience that I had with Jesus and the Holy Spirit before He sent me to India. I didn't realize it at the time, but the Lord was going to use me in a way that I had never been used before. I was very comfortable functioning prophetically in a church setting. I had experience leading various deliverance ministries, as well as development in the gifts of the Spirit. However, I had no idea that the Holy Spirit was going to shake up my whole world and shift my dependence from the church to Him and Him only, through dreams, visions and prophecy!

From 2014 through the Fall of 2015, I was spending a great deal of time in spiritual prayer, praying in the Holy Spirit. The season of praying in tongues columnated with the following dream that changed my life forever. The dream started with the Holy Spirit walking me out of my bedroom and leading me downstairs to my office. There was a young woman about twenty years old sitting at a desk to the right of the door of my office when I walked in. She was writing on paper. Jesus was standing adjacent to her and he said "*This is your great, great grandmother. You are the product of the prophetic vision that I gave her years ago and now is the time for this vision to bring life!*"

He then turned to the other side of the room where my desk was positioned. As He stepped toward my desk, He took the vision that I saw her writing on paper and placed it on my desk. He pulled out my chair and led me to sit at my desk. Jesus then touched a TV screen that was on the way and it came alive with different size crowds of foreign people. Crowds of hundreds, thousands, tens of thousands and even hundreds of thousands. He said to me *"prophesy what you see!"* I paused and then these words started to come out of my mouth. I said, *"The vision of the Lord Jesus Christ is that I am sent to the nations where I will bring the power of the Holy Spirit to the masses and they will pray in tongues and prophecy. Miracles, signs and wonders will happen to the people. There will be thousands upon thousands of pastors who are called into this mission and I will see the fruit of tens of thousands of pastors baptized in the Holy Ghost. Millions of people will receive the power of the Holy Spirit and pray in tongues."*

When I was finished, the Holy Spirit came into the room and stood beside me. Jesus placed a cloth over my shoulders. He then handed me a book. The book only had one page. Jesus opened the one page of the book and read the words to me. He said, *"Raise the dead, cast out devils, heal the sick, and baptize in the Holy Spirit!"* He then said, *"A man from India will call you...Go!"*

When I woke up, the hair on my arms was standing straight up and I was burning on the inside like fire. The dream was vivid. It was real. It was so real I was shaking. Jesus and the Holy Spirit visited me and had just called me to India and imparted something supernaturally to me in order to execute the vision. However, the reality was that I had no contacts in India and did not know anybody who ever went to India. However, none of that mattered. The only thing that mattered was that Jesus and the Holy Ghost called me to a nation.

Seven days after this dream, a man from India called me. Within six weeks, I was preaching in crusades on the other side of the world. Over the last four years, as of the writing of this book, I have preached to hundreds of thousands of people and seen so many miracles I cannot even count. However, the main purpose everywhere I go according to the call I described above, is to take the power of the Holy Spirit with the equipping of all the gifts of the Spirit. Especially the gift of tongues. Everywhere I go, people get baptized in the Holy Spirit and pray in tongues. This did not come from memorizing the Bible and endless hours of study, even though I have spent hundreds of hours in study. It came from Christ in a dream that imparted an ability to do something I could not do before this encounter.

My point in writing this book is that there are many who sit right now in dormant churches and do not know their real calling because they never received the Holy Spirit, or they never pursued the Holy Spirit with all their heart, mind and soul. I believe there is an impartation through this book that will open up the realm of the Holy Spirit and establish a heart cry through supplication and prayer that will shake the door of heaven and cause a release of the dreams and visions in the hearts of the reader.

## 6

# EXECUTE THE VISION

### WHAT DO YOU SEE?

Jeremiah 1:12 "Then the Lord said to me, "You have seen well, for I am ready to perform My word."

WHEN HOLY SPIRIT WAS PREPARING JEREMIAH TO DO A supernatural thing, He did not have him memorize his Bible (Torah) and then test him on it. What the Spirit did do was to impart the Holy Spirit to him and then verify the language in which Holy Spirit would speak to him. This direct voice of God to Jeremiah would be the foundation in which Jeremiah confronted the darkness, as well as the dead church. The majority of Jeremiah's ministry was spent weeping over the dead church. He didn't weep because of their acts of sin. The act of sin was just the product of not knowing God. The religious leaders went through the motions in the church with their rituals at the synagogue, while the entire nation rejected the face of God. In order to fulfill his call, Jeremiah would need absolute confidence in the instruction that the Spirit Himself gave to him. Only then would he be ready to do something that is impossible for a man, but supernaturally possible for a man who knows the Holy Spirit.

The way in which the Spirit prepared Jeremiah is by simply talking with him and verifying they spoke the same language. This heavenly language that is revealed through this communication sequence is simple, confirming alignment in purpose and who the audience is, as well as imparting faith. Lets look at Jeremiah 1:11-12, *"Moreover the word of the Lord came to me, saying, 'Jeremiah, what do you see?' And I said, 'I see a branch of an almond tree.' Then the Lord said to me, 'You have seen well, for I am ready to perform My word.'"* First, Holy Spirit establishes that He is speaking to Jeremiah in a form of pictures and visions. The vision was the prophetic words in picture form spoken by the Spirit which carry the power and glory of heaven.

The Spirit of God is bringing an intention from heaven to earth through a man to execute the vision and release heaven on earth. So, in this practice session, all the Spirit wants to confirm with Jeremiah is "what did you see?" The word "see" is the Hebrew word **Raah** meaning the vision or dream imparted to the mind of man by the Shepherd Himself. It is interesting to note that one of the names of God is **Jehovah-Raah** meaning *The Lord is my Shepherd.* Therefore, God is developing the shepherding process with Jeremiah.

The Spirit is teaching him to simply trust in what He is revealing to Jeremiah through vision and the Shepherd will lead the way. The Shepherd is making Himself so known to Jeremiah that his trust is not simply in a Bible where he has to interpret and try to apply meaning for people, time and place, but the

Spirit simplifies the relationship and establishes great authority in Jeremiah's life through direct and simple communication in the form of vision. The Spirit then confirms to Jeremiah saying "I will execute the vision."

Jeremiah only has to wait on the Shepherd and see visions/dreams from Him, and the Spirit is the one who executes (does the work). Afterwards, the Spirit confirms that Jeremiah knows the way in which He is communicating with him. The Spirit then gives him a vision of a boiling pot coming from the north (1 Jeremiah 1:13-19) and Jeremiah confirms what he sees. The Spirit then begins to explain the vision and positions him to speak (prophesy, teach, explain). In this same fashion, the Spirit calls sons and daughters to speak for Him and it is imperative that our churches are led by sons and daughters who hear the voice of the Holy Spirit and wait upon the vision.

Remember, it is Jesus who vowed to build His church. It is not man picking and choosing scripture out of the Bible randomly, thinking they are doing the right thing, in the right place, at the right time. Only the Holy Spirit identifies the right time, the right place with the right people. Anything that is not built on the voice of the Spirit will crumble and be blown away by the wind. This includes people who randomly choose scriptures but are not sent with specific vision and purpose. Randomly chosen scripture always has a twist because any motivation that is not of the Holy Spirit, but is man driven, will crumble and not multiply (Matthew 16:13-19, 1 Corinthians 3:10-23, 1 John 4:1).

I want to stress that numbers alone aren't evidence. Many false ministries have thousands of people following them, but the numbers are not the evidence. Sons and daughters walking in the power of the Holy Spirit with signs, wonders and miracles are the evidence. A man who multiples five sons in the Spirit is greater than a 10,000 member church where nobody hears the voice of God. It is not possible to know Christ and not multiply!

Once this revelation of *Jehovah Raah* enters your spirit, there should be great joy in the prophecy in *Joel 2:28*, *"And it shall come to pass afterward that I will pour out My Spirit on all flesh; Your sons and your daughters shall prophesy, Your old men shall dream dreams, Your young men shall see visions."* This prophecy is the promise of the outpouring of the Holy Spirit where the masses of believers who receive the baptism of the Holy Spirit will be equipped just like Jeremiah to be trained by *Jehovah Raah*. This is the vision of Christ. This is His view of the church in the new covenant. This is the way of the Spirit of God who was sent to the masses on the Day of Pentecost (Acts 2:17, 9:10, 10:3, 12:9, 16:9, 18:9, Revelation 1:9).

## THE CHURCH OF HOLY SPIRIT FIRE!

This way of the Spirit is the central theme in which Jesus declares He will build His church. *Ephesians 5:25-27, "Husbands, love your wives, just as Christ also loved the church and gave Himself for her, that He might sanctify and cleanse her with the washing of water by the word, that He might present her to Himself a glorious church, not having spot or wrinkle or any such thing, but that she should be holy and without blemish."* Pastors, church leaders, apostles, prophets, evangelists, no matter who you are, this understanding is necessary so that you do not repeat the errors of previous generations and simply shove the Bible down the throats of believers. Only the Spirit gives life.

Jesus came as a Lamb who was led by the Holy Spirit, and the voice of the Spirit came in visions and dreams that led Jesus to minister to thousands on one day, small groups on other days, and then single individuals in between. Each meeting had purpose and each encounter with the people was deliberate, having the specific intent of vision. This is a picture of what a true functioning church looks like: Family caring for each other and praying until vision ensures the deliverance, identification, equipping, and sending of people.

The true church is first family centered on the Spirit of God, and its organization is to be centered upon the hearing of the Holy Spirit. Doctrines were not meant to be what people gather around. The Holy Spirit's voice must be paramount with His nature of love and deliverance embodied by the people who gather around this fire.

When any organization centers upon doctrine, including biblical doctrine as the outline of the church - error, control and corruption will always follow. However, when the Holy Spirit is the central point and people are trained to discern the Spirit of God, their confidence is automatic, like Jeremiah, because they are trained to hear and see in the Spirit of God (vision, dreams and prophecy).

In verse 25 above, the first command is for leaders to love (agape) meaning to give their lives for the cause of Christ, the way Jesus gave His life for the church. It is not the personal desire of the minister, it's the minister's willingness to wait on the Spirit of God, see visions, and then *wash* the people (the bride). This is a Holy Ghost family picture. The vision (prophecy or dream) given to the minister for the people washes the bride.

Reading the Bible alone does not wash the bride. The Holy Spirit is personal and knows the needs of the people. True *Apostolic design* centers on *washing the bride,* meaning ministers are called to give their lives (their will) to God, listen for the voice of the Spirit and give specific ministry to specific people or groups of people. This is what *washing the bride* means. It releases the direct voice of God to the right people, in the right place, at the right time. It is the vision that carries supernatural power to impart something from heaven to the person (people).

"Word" in verse 25 is the word *rhema,* meaning the direct voice of God (dream, vision or prophecy) and is what washes the people (person) and cleanses the soul through the release of the heart of Jesus on earth. In essence, the revelation of the power of the Spirit that Paul was trying to portray to the Ephesians was that prophecy (visions and dreams) washes the hearts of the people because it is the direct word of Christ specific to that time and place and intent. The Spirit will oftentimes use scriptures to expand understanding and bring continual deliverance.

The Bible should be the reference when the Holy Spirit is teaching, as He will often bring revelation of scripture, but the Bible is the reference, which is revealed by the Spirit. Living water flows from the Spirit, connecting vision and dreams oftentimes to the scriptures. But you must know this, God is so much bigger than the Bible. He is infinite and knows all things.

The last thing we should do is limit God to the written scriptures. The Lord calling me to India was not in the Bible. He used scriptures to support my calling, but I had to believe His direct voice, His vision and walk into the unknown trusting the Spirit. The true shepherd (pastor, apostle, prophet, evangelist, teacher) is so submitted to the Shepherd, that living water is what flows from the mouth of *Jehovah Raah* to the bride, washing the church in the power of the Spirit!

~

## GETTING BACK TO THE QUESTION: CAN THE BIBLE BE PHILOSOPHY?

When Paul was sent to Athens by the Holy Ghost, Paul recognized that he was dealing with the most philosophical people on earth and therefore he did not pull out a Bible and try to begin explaining scriptures to people because that is not the way of the Spirit. Not only that, the Greeks were professionals at rationalization so they could recognize wise discussion. Paul realized if he ended up debating with them, the Bible in their perspective, could just be another book written by a wise man like Socrates or Plato.

Paul's goal was not to introduce the Greeks to the Bible. In fact, the Bible (New Testament) was not even written at the time of Paul. Paul's goal was to introduce the Greeks to the living God, testifying of His presence. Led by the Holy Spirit, Paul says in the book of *1 Corinthians 2:1-5*, *"And I, brethren, when I came to you, did not come with excellence of speech or of wisdom declaring to you the testimony of God. For I determined not to know anything among you except Jesus Christ and Him crucified. I was with you in weakness, in fear, and in much trembling. And my speech and my preaching were not with persuasive words of human wisdom, but in demonstration of the Spirit and of power,* **that your faith should not be in the wisdom of men but in the power of God."**

Paul went directly to the power of the Holy Ghost and illustrated the kingdom with words of knowledge, prophecy, the working of miracles, signs and wonders and he ministered to Plato's great-great-great grandchildren...

The Corinthians were not won over by Paul's philosophical understanding of the Bible and his ability to articulate it well or preach like one of the great preachers of that time. They were won over by the Spirit of God when Paul read their hearts and prophesied causing men to fall down and declare Jesus Christ is Lord as the secrets of their hearts were revealed. Words of knowledge produced miracles before their eyes. The conversion of the Greeks was the work of the Spirit who led a man named Paul by visions and supernatural direction of the Holy Spirit. This was not the work of a man who just went and read the Bible to the Greeks.

## GO, GIVE THE VISION!

Long before the call to India, The Spirit of God taught me a lesson of the power of vision that changed my life forever. It literally was a paradigm shift from being Bible focused and working to understand it, versus trusting in the Holy Spirit and being led to do what He shows me.

In 2009, I became disgusted with witnessing because I was not seeing much fruit and it was very discouraging. I had purchased some popular videos that described how to use scripture and lead people to the revelation that they were a sinner and needed to meet Jesus. I did this for a while but it never really produced much of anything other than frustration. Over time, I got discouraged and started to question Jesus a lot because something had to be wrong. I stopped witnessing to people and started asking questions to the Holy Spirit. It was probably one of the greatest turning points in my walk with Christ.

One morning I woke early and went to get my coffee and go down to my office for normal prayer. The Lord began speaking to me in very clear voice saying, "Go to Panera for lunch." So, having been given this instruction, I went to Panera, a local restaurant, and sat by the door. On this particular day, the restaurant was full with few seats available for people.

As I was sitting there on the couch, a young woman about 21 years old walked through the door. Immediately the Lord began speaking to me about this young girl. He gave me a vision for her and instructed me to tell her its meaning. It was a vision and a prophecy of her having great influence on the younger generation as a gift from God and that she would raise up so many sons and daughters that she would change the landscape in the place where she lives. I said ok and watched her order, get her food, and to my amazement, find a seat at a table that was right behind the couch where I was seated. I was shocked. Not only did the Lord speak to me specifically about her, but He positioned me in the very spot necessary for me to hear the context of the condition of her heart.

As I sat there minding my own business, she came and sat with a young man who turned out to be a pastor at another local church. She started talking with the pastor, revealing in her discussion with him that she was an intern at a denominational church and that she was so disheartened at what she saw happening behind the scenes at this local church that she was ready to quit her internship and walk away from church, along with everything that goes with church.

At this moment, I felt the unction of the Holy Spirit and I introduced myself. I told her that I had a prophecy from the Holy Spirit for her and began to share. It only took a minute, but it is a minute that I will never ever forget. Her eyes welled up with tears so big that they bounced off the table. Her head suddenly fell forward and she literally fell into her salad. She was weeping uncontrollably. Every person in Panera was now looking, so the pastor and I picked her up and we took her outside where we got her into the pastor's car. He said he was going to take her back to her room on campus at the local college, so I left and returned to work.

I jumped into my car and began rejoicing, but little did I know that this was only the beginning of what the Lord was teaching me about the power of a vision and the impact of prophecy. At the end of the day, I got in my car and drove to my local gym like I always do. I walked through the door and there was a guy named Chris who I knew on the other side of the gym. He started screaming my name and telling me to come and hear a story.

As I got closer, I could see there was a young man sitting with his back against the wall and it was evident that he had been crying. He looked like a deer in the headlights. Chris started to explain that this young man spent all afternoon in a young girl's dorm room. The reason he was there, was that he was called by friends to come and see what was happening in her dorm room. Chris went on to say that this young man said that a man named David prophesied over this girl at Panera and when the pastor brought her back to her room she laid on the floor and the glory of God became so heavy that every person who came into the room fell down and began to weep like this young man is doing now. Chris said this young man explained that there were dozens and dozens of people as word spread across campus to come and see what was happening. Apparently this went on all afternoon and there were people still on the floor in her dorm room, weeping just like this young man who was experiencing the presence of the Holy Spirit to such a degree that every five minutes he fell down and started weeping again.

Many lives were changed that day. There were young

students calling me and asking what happened. Why? What is this thing called the Holy Spirit? Why could I not stop weeping and shaking? This experience of the glory of God is something that changed many people's lives that day. Two young men quit school and signed up for Bethel's Supernatural School of Ministry in Redding CA. One of those young men became a pastor and resides in Germany. Countless students had their lives changed in one afternoon. To this day, I still have people come up to me and say they know of someone who was there and this is what happened...

My frustration with an *old-school approach* to witnessing resulted in questions to the Holy Spirit that simplified my path of life. The call to India and what I do in that nation is centered on the prophetic hearing of the voice of the Holy Spirit and awakening pastors and leaders in that nation to the power of the Holy Spirit.

Needless to say, I learned firsthand about the power of prophecy and why the Lord gives vision. He desires that heaven invade earth. He desires that we stop mucking things up with dead religious forms of witnessing and trying to shove the Bible down peoples' throats. Instead, all we need is a vision and He promises to unleash the glory of God upon this earth, doing things that we cannot imagine and things that are so supernatural, that the witness will truly be the witness of the power of the Spirit of God and not from the work of our own desires.

7
———

# BLOWN BY THE WIND

## THE NEW BREED

> I Corinthians 12:1 "Now concerning spiritual gifts, brethren, I do not want you to be ignorant."

AFTER JESUS SPENT TIME SHAKING UP THE RELIGIOUS SYSTEM OF the day, as God confirmed the prophetic visions and prophecy spoken by Christ with confirming miracles, signs and wonders, even the Pharisees recognized that Jesus was functioning under an authority that was not of this world (Matthew 7:29, Mark 11:28). The Pharisees and Sadducees knew the word of the Bible, but Jesus walked in an authority that was beyond the Bible. The authority was from another realm, the realm of heaven. This contrast between the Pharisees and Sadducees who knew the words on paper, but not the Living Word standing in front of them epitomizes the vast contrast between life in the Spirit versus Bible-readers. Jesus wasn't *just* a Bible-reader and student of the Law. He walked in the Spirit of Life. The contrast was so great that the Bible-readers crucified the living Christ. Jesus looked nothing like them because He functioned by the Spirit, while the Pharisees and Sadducees functioned by the letter of the written word interpreted through man's broken heart. However, even the Pharisees and Sadducees were astounded by the power of the Spirit. Many of them in private were questioning everything.

That is what the supernatural does in religious environments. The supernatural power of the Spirit reveals the fake and establishes those under the authority of the Spirit of God's vision. Nicodemus was one of these such men who came to Jesus privately and asked about this new way that Christ was demonstrating and teaching versus the old way of the Pharisees and Sadducees built on the inadequate covenant of the Law of Moses. *John 3:3-8, "Jesus answered and said to him, 'Most assuredly, I say to you, unless one is born again, he cannot see the kingdom of God.' Nicodemus said to Him, 'How can a man be born when he is old? Can he enter a second time into his mother's womb and be born?' Jesus answered, 'most assuredly, I say to you, unless one is born of water and the Spirit, he cannot enter the kingdom of God. That which is born of the flesh is flesh, and that which is born of the Spirit is spirit. Do not marvel that I said to you, You must be born again. The wind blows where it wishes, and you hear the sound of it, but cannot tell where it comes from and where it goes. So is everyone who is born of the Spirit.'"*

Nicodemus was blown away with the concept of being born again. He was not able to understand it, but recognized that something new was being offered. Jesus blew his mind saying that *your spirit must be reborn.* Jesus was basically saying that right now, Nicodemus, your spirit is entombed by your soul that's been captured by the darkness of this world, and the Law of Moses that you settled for, because the Law of Moses is unable to give your spirit new life and open up your soul to the King of Glory! Jesus was saying that He holds the power to break through this entombment, birthing your spirit from death, and saving your soul.

The same picture of Jesus Christ being resurrected from the grave, is a picture of a person's soul being opened by Jesus the Breaker (Micah 2:13) and being born again in the Spirit to spirit contact (the Holy Spirit with your spirit). This is resurrection power. Jesus closes the deal by revealing the new operating system. This totally shakes the mind of Nicodemus that was built upon dead religion. Jesus was saying that the performance of rituals was given because you are locked in a tomb (your soul is locked entombing your spirit and you are bound by the covenant of death – Hebrews 9:15). Jesus was saying essentially, *the authority you recognize, Nicodemus, is that of the Mediator of the new covenant that will establish a new breed of believers who will not be bound by words on stone, but by the living works Christ speaks (writes) on the hearts of men. When I speak, Nicodemus, the hearts of men will be moved by the wind of the Holy Spirit. It is the Spirit that you are recognizing that is different from your religious system.*

Wow! Wow! Wow! Thank you Jesus! Not only for the cross, but for the cross and the resurrection, because you fulfilled the Law of Moses and its debt, but you also resurrected us in the power of the Holy Spirit.

The baptism of the power of the Holy Spirit is so important for this reason. There is no legitimate moving of the hearts of men without the direct voice of God through the wind of the Holy Spirit. It is the engine by which the spirit of men is brought to life and is resurrected to hear the voice of God directly. The picture of the mighty rushing wind on the day of Pentecost was actually the required second piece of the new covenant. The death of Christ breaks open the tomb of the soul, but the mighty rushing wind births the spirit of men, mixing completely and equipping sons and daughters to hear the voice of God directly. This is the answer to Nicodemus' question and the answer to turning a church that is powerless into a church of power, because when the mighty rushing wind comes, the pattern is always tongues and then prophecy (Acts 2:1-18, Acts 19:1-7, I Corinthians 14).

## SPIRITUAL BLINDNESS OR THE VOICE OF GOD?

The reason Nicodemus was shaken on the inside was that he recognized that in their old religious routines, there was no authority, no life and no resurrection. There was no power, only submission to a system that drove condemnation. There was no voice of God. It was simply ritual performance. Any authority the Pharisees and Sadducees tried to execute, was a false authority built upon twisting the scriptures giving the people the appearance that the Pharisees and Sadducees were unique and special in the eyes of God. This was fake authority used to control the people, not liberate them like the heart of Christ.

True authority from Christ always liberates and empowers the people to hear His voice and follow. Fake authority always controls and keeps people inside the walls of an organization. Jesus actually confronted this false operating system with great anger and indignation (Matthew 23:1-36). Jesus revealed that they were, "Sons of Satan, a brood of vipers, whitewashed tombs and dead men's bones." You see, these men thought they were alive because of the system they followed using the written scriptures as their means of justification, saying it was from God. But Jesus reveals, as we discussed in previous chapters, that they did not have His living word (His voice) abiding in them (John 5:38). They had memorized scriptures, but they were entombed by death (Hebrews 9) because the Spirit (the Wind) was not present to roll-away the stone and open their souls to the King of Glory. They could not hear the voice of God. Their refusal of the Holy Spirit made them walking tombs and dead men's bones as they rejected the way of the Spirit.

Paul makes an explicit demand upon the church in *1 Corinthians 12:1, "Now concerning spiritual gifts, brethren, I do not want you to be ignorant."* The word "gifts" is italicized in this scripture because it was added to help explain the word "spiritual" as it requires additional explanation to understand its meaning in the English language. The Greek word for spirituals is the word **pneumatikos** meaning *wind* or *to be moved by the wind.*

Paul is saying, remember the words of Jesus Christ in His explanation to Nicodemus that our churches are to be centered on this new operating system so that we would have the direct living spoken words of the Spirit, and not just words on paper. Our churches are to be built based on the relationship of hearing the voice of the God and expecting Jesus Himself to build the church just as He decreed in Matthew 16:13-19. Paul goes on to explain that when the wind blows, and visions and dreams come to people, it will manifest in the church through the following demonstrations of power, *1 Corinthians 12:4-11 "There are diversities of gifts, but the same Spirit. There are differences of ministries, but the same Lord. And there are diversities of activities, but it is the same God who works all in all. But the manifestation of the Spirit is given to each one for the profit of all: for to one is given the word of wisdom through the Spirit, to another the word of knowledge through the same Spirit, to another faith by the same Spirit, to another gifts of healing by the same Spirit, to another the working of miracles, to another prophecy, to another discerning of spirits, to another different kinds of tongues, to another the interpretation of tongues. But one and the same Spirit works all these things, distributing to each one individually as He wills."*

Pay close attention to verse 11. It is the will of the Spirit to establish the means of manifestation of life giving resurrection power, but the communication process is the same. The Spirit speaks through dreams and visions, and people are positioned by the Spirit to prophecy, reveal words of knowledge, to pray for healing, to discern a situation or evil spirit, to give a tongue and/or interpret the tongue. The same Holy Spirit is the driving wind in the church! The wind of the Spirit is the engine. Without the engine, there is no power. No matter how much scripture you read, without the wind of the Holy Spirit, churches remain powerless and will not reproduce. Worse yet, many who think they are alive because they read the Bible and do "good works", unfortunately are dead because they reject the Holy Spirit.

Notice Jesus' warning to the church of Sardis. He says *"And to the angel of the church in Sardis write, 'These things says He who has the seven Spirits of God and the seven stars: I know your works, that you have a name that you are alive, but you are dead (Revelation 3:1).'"*

The church appeared righteous in doing good works and had a respectable reputation in the community, but was dead because they lacked the Spirit. This is the same point of Paul's discussion of the gifts of the Holy Spirit. Embracing the gifts and flow of the Holy Spirit is the way to life in the church because the Spirit gives life (Zechariah 4:6, 2 Corinthians 3:4-6).

# THE RESTORATION OF RIGHTEOUS JUDGMENT TO THE CHURCH

*Isaiah 11:1-3, "There shall come forth a Rod from the stem of Jesse, And a Branch shall grow out of his roots. The Spirit of the Lord shall rest upon Him, The Spirit of wisdom and understanding, The Spirit of counsel and might, The Spirit of knowledge and of the fear of the Lord. His delight is in the fear of the Lord, And He shall not judge by the sight of His eyes, Nor decide by the hearing of His ears; But with righteousness He shall judge the poor, and decide with equity for the meek of the earth; He shall strike the earth with the rod of His mouth, and with the breath of His lips He shall slay the wicked.*

It takes guts to love like Jesus. Jesus didn't look like the church of the day! He was persecuted by those most zealous in the letter of the written word. But that didn't stop Jesus. He found life in the Spirit, not in the honor of men. He dwelled in the Spirit and He did what He saw His Father do in spiritual prayer (John 5:19). This resulted in the dead being raised, the blind made to see, the deaf made to hear, the lame leaping and the power of the Holy Spirit being given to all who believed. Please take note, that the Spirit of Knowledge rested upon Jesus.

The Hebrew word for knowledge in this scripture is the Hebrew word **Yada** meaning intimacy, and is the same word used to describe when Adam and Eve came to together to produce sons and daughters. This same word description for spiritual intimacy also has roots in the description of creation when it says that the Spirit hovered and the Lord spoke (Genesis 1:1-3). The living voice is the only power that creates, and a believer is offered to be clothed in the Spirit of Knowledge or Intimacy (**Yada**), releasing the same creative power of the direct voice of God. This is the source of true prophecy, the Spirit of

Prophecy. True prophecy judges darkness and in righteousness creates the new man.

When you are in relationship with the Spirit of God and you hear His voice through dreams and visions, He is giving you authorization to announce His vision, which He creates before your eyes. The reason why there is very little creation (birthing of new things) in American churches is they have rationalized away the Spirit of God, defaulting solely to written scriptures. They rationalize away the reality of not seeing miracles because they have eliminated the very thing needed to produce life, and that is intimacy with the Holy Spirit. Better yet, to describe the *Yada* Jesus had with the knowledge of God, He fully demonstrated as a son that through relationship with the Father, their regular communication through visions, dreams and the unction of the Spirit, created life.

This is spiritual intimacy. Jesus didn't look like the church of the day who performed routines and rituals, He looked like something that was out of this world because He was fueled by something they rejected, *Yada* with the Spirit of God. Therefore, when He judged in righteousness, meaning He sought the Spirit and the Spirit led Him with vision and the direct voice of God, the result was miracles, signs and wonders. The darkness all around Him was judged continually releasing life and resurrection power everywhere He walked. What if our churches were fueled by the Spirit of Knowledge? As referenced in the previous chapter, true spiritual knowledge is revealed through the vision of the Spirit, the result of intimacy with the Spirit (Isaiah 28:9-12).

It takes the intimacy of the Holy Spirit to fuel a confidence that is not of this world. We talked in a previous chapter about how Paul took the time in Ephesians 3 to distinguish between earthly knowledge versus supernatural knowledge from heaven coming from visions and dreams. Supernatural knowledge of the Spirit doesn't just happen, it is the product of intimacy with the Holy Spirit. There is a great void today in the church for the power of the Spirit and the root cause is a lack of intimacy with the Holy Spirit. The design of God, through Jesus Christ, is to rebuild the tent of David. Those who are so in love with the Holy Spirit, that they dwell together with the Holy Spirit and the living voice of God. Through this love, life flows to the people of the world.

The centerpiece of the gifts of the Holy Spirit is supernatural *agape* love. Paul explains in 1 Corinthians 13 that love is the fiery passion that must fuel our hearts with purpose. Any lack of vision is directly connected to the state of intimacy and expectancy of the Christ. The church today does not lack Bible readers. The church today lacks sons and daughters of God who are willing to bring righteous judgment to the church and to the world through the love of God they carry in their heart. True boldness comes from those who dwell in the shadow of His wings like David. The church is in dire need of the *Davids*.

## THE RIGHTEOUS JUDGE

So what is real righteous judgment? Let me first say what it is *not*. True righteous judgment is not fueled by condemnation and accusation. Those are the nature of the evil one. Instead, true righteous judgment is fueled by passionate love that was sent to deliver sons and daughters into the kingdom of heaven. The nature of this intimate love was portrayed by Jesus Himself after He was baptized in the Holy Spirit. The Bible says that Jesus went into the synagogue and declared the nature of the One sent to deliver the nations, quoting *Isaiah 61:1 (Luke 4:18-19)*, *"The Spirit of the Lord God is upon me, because the Lord has anointed and qualified me to preach the Gospel of good tidings to the meek, the poor, and afflicted; He has sent me to bind up and heal the brokenhearted, to proclaim liberty to the [physical and spiritual] captives and the opening of the prison and of the eyes to those who are bound, to proclaim the FAVOR of the Lord and the day of vengeance of our God, to comfort all who mourn..."*

Jesus came to deliver people from the tomb of death, fulfilling the very thing that the Law of Moses could not do. His nature is *for man* and not *against man*.

One of my favorite scriptures reveals the heart of God for humanity. It is the description of the view from heaven for those bound in sin and death, and is found in *Isaiah 59:15-20*, *"Then the Lord saw it, and it displeased Him that there was no justice. He saw that there was no man, And wondered that there was no intercessor (AVENGER); Therefore His own arm brought salvation for Him; And His own righteousness, it sustained Him. For He put on righteousness as a breastplate, And a helmet of salvation on His head; He put on the garments of vengeance for clothing, And was clad with zeal as a cloak. According to their deeds, accordingly He will repay, Fury to His adversaries, Recompense to His enemies..."*

Take note that Jesus looked from heaven, driven to fulfill the call to come to earth and redeem mankind. This is His heart which burns with zeal and vengeance to deliver you and bring judgment against the darkness that deceived Adam all the way back in Eden. The word recompense means to treat a person with justice and to stand with a person against an enemy. This is a covenant promise because the Father sees you innocent through the blood of Jesus. This is the heart of a *sent one* by Christ. Willing to die for the harvest of souls.

This not only includes the nations, but the call of avenging deceptive, dead religion which throttles dead churches which are more connected to political correctness and dead religious systems. Much of the church has been castrated because righteous judgment has been made into a curse word, wrongly defined by people who function under the Law of Moses instead of the Law of the Spirit (Romans 8:2). Let me tell you something, righteous judgment is the only means by which truth is brought to a blinded heart. True righteous judgment is rooted in delivering the captives, opening the prison doors and bringing sight to the blind.

When churches relegate the Spirit of God as a "bolt on option" or even rationalize why the voice of God is not needed, the people stay blinded in their hearts (Matthew 15:1-13). These blinded hearts of men are not connected directly with the burning heart of Christ, unable to hear His voice in dreams and visions because they have been made deaf by religion and political correctness, castrating them without them even knowing it. This is the great deception. But God is raising up those who hear His voice to righteously judge in the church and bring deliverance to the people. The true Shepherds are being awakened by the Holy Spirit in a new measure of Spirit leadership in the realm of deliverance through the gifts of the Holy Spirit.

## WHAT DOES THE INVASION LOOK LIKE?

Many people look at the book of Revelation as an end time book and there are parts of it that tell of future events. However, prophecy is always multidimensional and can have applications in real time as well as in the future. I believe Revelation 19:11-15 is one of those scriptures. What is described is the Word of God, the very person of Christ, who speaks, coming out of heaven with the army of the Lord to fulfill visions, dreams and prophecy.

*Revelation 19:11-15 "...Now I saw heaven opened, and behold, a white horse. And He who sat on him was called Faithful and True, and in righteousness He judges and makes war. His eyes were like a flame of fire, and on His head were many crowns. He had a name written that no one knew except Himself. He was clothed with a robe dipped in blood, and **His name is called The Word of God.** And the armies in heaven, clothed in fine linen, white and clean, followed Him on white horses. Now out of His mouth goes a sharp sword, that with it He should strike the nations. And He Himself will rule them with a rod of iron. He Himself treads the winepress of the fierceness and wrath of Almighty God. And He has on His robe and on His thigh a name written: KING OF KINGS AND LORD OF LORDS."*

When you start seeing dreams and visions on a consistent basis, prepare yourself because the Spirit of God is training you to invade a home, a workplace, a church, a city or even a nation. To judge righteously by declaring His vision. You better believe that that vision is not simply a fictitious, non-purposed pizza dream. It is the key of David that carries the government of God, equipping you to walk into a place and open a door of restoration that all of heaven is behind the vision because it is the WORD of God (Christ Himself) and it comes with many crowns, eyes of fire, a sword, a robe dipped in blood riding a white horse. Your confidence must be in the vision that does not exist yet, but you are willing to prophesy the vision knowing that the rider of the white horse has come to invade the earth!

This is the Spirit of Prophecy, Revelations 19:10 *"...for Jesus Christ is the Spirit of Prophecy."* Notice that the word prophecy in that scripture is capitalized meaning it is reflective of Jesus

Christ Himself, the person of Christ. A person who prophesies the vision of the Lord is releasing Christ Himself into the situation and is bringing light into the darkness. My confidence is in none other than Jesus Christ, the Spirit of Prophecy. I have stood in front of crowds of thousands, in front of company presidents and people on their deathbed with cancer. However, by the vision of the Spirit of Prophecy, I have seen those thousands of people come to the altar and be baptized in the Holy Ghost, presidents weep and receive Jesus because I shared a dream, and even people with final stages of lung cancer, who heard me speak the vision of seeing the hand of God removing their cancer, resulting in them being made whole (cancer free) because of the vision. This is true prophecy fueled by the vision releasing the rider of the white horse out of heaven, the true living WORD OF GOD! I believe this is what Jesus meant when said *"thy kingdom come, your will be done, on earth as it is in heaven (Mathew 6:10)!"*

## GOD OF THE IMPOSSIBLE

When I go to India, I preach sometimes 5-6 times a day to crowds ranging is size from 100 to 10,000 people. I have learned to wait on the Spirit for vision, directing me. Sometimes all I do is prophesy and people get healed, tumors fall off and thousands receive the power of the Holy Spirit and speak in tongues. However, the story I am about to tell you stretched my faith in His vision beyond imagination.

My contact picked me up from the hotel one evening in a city on the east central east coast in India. I asked where we were going because we were so busy going from church to church during the day that I hadn't even bothered to ask. So, the Indian

Pastor replies, *I am taking you to a "special" village.* I said ok and didn't think much about it. About an hour later, exhausted but yet excited for what the Holy Spirit was going to do that evening, I started getting this weird feeling in my Spirit. I asked the pastor for answers and he said that we are going to a village that is 100% followers of the snake god. They worship the cobra. They hate Christians and have been known to hurt them.

So, a logical question came flying out of my mouth, "Why are we going to this place?" He turned around from the passenger seat and looked me in the eyes with this mischievous grin on his face and said, "We told them you do magic tricks!" I'm not sure what I looked like, but if it was what I was feeling inside I probably turned white as a sheet. I said "What? Magic tricks?" He giggled and said "Yes, magic tricks." I sat there for a few minutes and said "So what do you mean?" He giggled even harder. At this point I'm kind of irritated because I'm thinking this is real and we could die. He was still giggling in the front seat. I guess he had more confidence in me and the Holy Spirit at that time than I did. Who would be so brave as to enter the "snake pit" without a plan? I sat back and listened for the Holy Spirit. The Holy Spirit showed me a vision of a young girl with two ponytails and a blue polka-dot dress in the third row. I'll never forget it because the picture of this girl is etched in my mind. My whole life at this point now depends on us walking in and me seeing this girl sitting in the third row.

We arrive and it feels like I there is a lump in my throat so big that I can't swallow. I had ministered hundreds of times in India prior to this event and yet this felt scarier than when I got off the plane the first time. However, somehow, I got enough strength in my legs to get out of the car and walk into the tent. There were about 600 people sitting in this place waiting to be entertained by a magician. By the grace of God, as we are walking on stage, I saw the girl the Holy Spirit showed me in the vision. The young girl with two ponytails and a blue polka-dot dress was in the third row. I'm so thankful at this point. I had no idea what was going to happen next but at least I knew the Holy Spirit now had a plan centered around this young girl. Think about this because if you are reading this book, I believe you will also find yourself one day in a situation like this, possibly with an Indian who has crazy faith and an even more crazy American ready and willing to be vulnerable and do something supernatural for Christ.

A few different speakers said a few things and suddenly I am introduced, and I have the mic in my hands. When I stand up, this amazing peace, like a hot warm blanket comes down over me. I started to talk, asking the girl from the third row with the blue polka-dot dress if she will come up and assist me.  She stands up and I ask to touch her forehead, so the interpreter asks her and she nods her head *yes*. I raise my arm and lay my left hand on her forehead. She falls down like a load of bricks. She hits the floor and lays their motionless. The crowd literally, in unison, gasps and stands up at the same time, to see her lying on the floor. They look at me with wide eyes and stand there looking at me as if are saying, "Wow that was one heck of a magic trick!"

I have to admit, I was as much in shock as they were, not only that she is laying there motionless on the floor in the Spirit, but that I have 600 people who I know are snake worshippers and hate Christians, staring at me and thinking that I possibly hurt one of their children. If you can picture this, it would be hard enough if I knew their language, but I did not speak their language. The mother of the child suddenly becomes very apparent to me as this woman starts screaming at me and runs up in front beside her daughter. She grabs the child's arm and starts pulling on her and screaming, doing everything she can think of, including slapping her in the face, trying to wake her up.

I looked at my interpreter (the giggling pastor) and suddenly these words started flowing out of my mouth describing how the Holy Spirit speaks to people in dreams and visions. The mom starts to calm down a little because she can tell that I am suddenly confident in describing what is happening to her. I spend the next twenty minutes, with this child still lying on the floor, under the power of the Spirit. I start describing the resurrection power of Jesus Christ. It was almost like the shock of the girl lying on the floor allowed me to talk about Jesus Christ to people who would never even entertain the notion of listening to somebody talk about Jesus Christ. It was like I had a captive audience. I had a revelation at this moment. Only God could get me into a place to minister to people that would normally want to hurt Christians.

After twenty minutes, with this girl still on the floor, I didn't know how this was going to end so I kept talking and explaining the power of Jesus Christ. What happened next even shocked me. As I am talking, the crowd suddenly gasped again so I turn around and find that the girl has stood up. She is shaking and asking to speak to the people. She starts to talk her native language, and the interpreter is telling me what she is saying. She begins by saying that she was taken to heaven and met a man named Jesus Christ. She says that Jesus hugged her, explained many things to her, and told her He is the Savior of the world, that He loves her, and that He is the only true God.

She then says that Jesus instructed her to tell the people about Him.

She handed the mic back to me and she walked back to her chair. I asked if anybody wanted to receive the power of the Holy Spirit and meet this God named Jesus. The whole crowd came forward and I was able to pray for them. I have seen many supernatural things in the mission field with thousands of people erupting in the gift of tongues for the first time, demonized people suddenly delivered, people crippled in wheelchairs suddenly standing up and walking, but to this day, this remains to me a sign and a wonder that can only be explained as, *"but God!"* To walk into a place with 600 people that would hurt you at the very least, and have to trust the Holy Spirit through this personal encounter process between Jesus and this one girl, and having it end up with hundreds of people weeping, hugging me and praying in tongues, is absolutely one of the craziest things I have ever experienced with the Holy Spirit.

# 8

# GIANT KILLERS

## KNOWING THE ENCOURAGER

1 Samuel 17:40 "Then he took his staff in his hand; and he chose for himself five smooth stones from the brook, and put them in a shepherd's bag, in a pouch which he had, and his sling was in his hand. And he drew near to the Philistine."

I WANT TO ESTABLISH A DISTINCTION IN THIS CHAPTER BETWEEN the real anointing and an imposter. There is a difference between those following the voice of the living God versus those adhering to a system that appears righteous and popular, but never takes down giants, hiding inside of walls of places we call churches. The fake are exposed when giants show up on the scene. To Illustrate this distinction, I want to share a dream the Lord gave me when He was transitioning me from being system dependent, to being dependent upon the voice of the Holy Spirit.

In this dream, I was visited by an angel who spoke to me and said "The Encourager" wants to speak with you. The angel walked me to a door and opened it. He led me inside where there was a tremendous glory light that was so bright there were no walls in the room, it was endless glory. There were two tables in front of me. On one table was a Bible and a container of Kool-Aid. On the other table was bread and wine. Jesus came out of the glory on a white horse and positioned Himself beside the bread and wine. He was glorious, and I saw written upon Him, **The Word of God** (Revelation 19:10-15). He said, *"I have come to encourage you in the clarity between the living and the dead. Life only comes from communion with Me."* Obviously, Jesus is saying, *"Don't drink the Kool-Aid, but drink My wine and eat My bread."*

*John 6:45-53 "It is written in the Prophets, 'And they shall all be taught by God.' Therefore everyone who has heard and learned from the Father comes to Me. Not that anyone has seen the Father, except He who is from God; He has seen the Father. Most assuredly, I say to you, he who believes in Me has everlasting life. I am the bread of life. Your fathers ate the manna in the wilderness, and are dead. This is the bread which comes down from heaven, that one may eat of it and not die. I am the living bread which came down from heaven. If anyone eats of this bread, he will live forever; and the bread that I shall give is My flesh, which I shall give for the life of the world." The Jews therefore quarreled among themselves, saying, 'How can this Man give us His flesh to eat?' Then Jesus said to them, 'Most assuredly, I say to you, unless you eat the flesh of the Son of Man and drink His blood, you have no life in you.'"*

The vision of the two tables reveals true communion which results in power, versus the table that is powerless, the Bible mixed with Kool-Aid (philosophy). The Bible was never meant to be a *pick and choose* menu selection which grants men the will to pick and choose belief systems and portions of the Bible. The way of true communion with the Spirit of God results in hearing His voice, bringing the risen Christ through dreams and visions and encounters into your life situations, for you and the people around you.

When the real Christ appears on the scene, either in your own prayer life, church, ministry, or home, there is an outpouring of the power of the Holy Spirit which is the evidence of His presence. This is the promise! The other table was a table of philosophy using the Bible as a deceptive Kool-Aid which produces a political system instead of a relation-driven life with the Holy Spirit. The Bible is not the issue since it is 100% true. The issue is the false motives of those interpreting the Bible. These motives typically manifest in places of powerlessness. No miracles, signs wonders, dreams, prophecy or visions, but a whole lot of philosophical use of the Bible as bait. Jesus again in John 6 distinguishes Himself as the living bread (the One who speaks to sons and daughters through communion – eating His bread and drinking His blood). He emphatically emphasizes that He is different from the manna in the wilderness (which is symbolizing the Law of Moses) declaring again that these words on stone produced death.

Again, when Jesus declares He will build His church and the gates of hell will not prevail (Matthew 16:13-19), He is declaring that He will speak directly to sons and daughters who are given to His way of the Spirit and signs and wonders will follow (Mark 16:15-18). Life does not come from an altar call and a self-proclaimed decision which is centered on picking and choosing scriptures out of the Bible. True life comes to a heart that listens to the voice of God because it is the voice of God which releases transforming power into the hearts of men, and through the transformed hearts of sons and daughters to the masses of people. The souls of men are supernaturally changed through the creator's voice (dreams, visions and prophecy) that causes the darkness to flee and reforms the soul.

## GIVE ME THE BREAD AND THE WINE

In the Story of David and Goliath, King Saul plays a major role in the contrast of understanding the difference between one who sits at the table with bread and wine versus the one who appears righteous, but is really a Kool-Aid drinker. Saul was a man chosen by God to be a king and Saul started out listening to the voice of God (the bread and wine), but something happened in having to deal with the pressure of leadership. Saul chose the popularity of the people and his reputation instead of adhering to the voice of God. When Saul started to make decisions without God, the Lord tore His Kingdom from Saul's hand and took away His Holy Spirit (1 Samuel 15:11-33).

The result was a man whom the Lord had chosen, but then lost the anointing of the Holy Spirit because of disobedience to the voice with the Holy Spirit. Saul made the relationship about his own personal desire which was twisted in needing to appease the desire of the people. He was worried about the numbers and who would follow him. In essence, Saul's selfish motive was exposed when the direct voice of the Lord instructed him to go and utterly destroy King Agag and all of the Amalekites. The people wanted something different and Saul tried to appease the people and God at the same time, which is not possible. Kingdoms do not function through conscious agreement with all the people involved. Kingdoms function when kings rule in righteousness. One King, One voice!

As Saul found out, the result was his spiritual death. Saul continued in the biblical ritual of tabernacle worship, building his own altar, having an appearance of righteousness because it was aligned with the Torah's altar requirements, but it was Kool-Aid for Saul and the people. Saul appeared to still be "the king" but was now just a figurehead because the Lord sought for a man after His own heart, who would drink the wine and eat the bread from the table of the Lord Jesus. This is the only table capable to equip a man to do impossible things like slaying giants.

Saul revealed the condition of his heart prior to this incident with the Amalekites.

*1 Samuel 13:7-14, "As for Saul, he was still in Gilgal, and all the people followed him trembling. Then he waited seven days, according to the time set by Samuel. But Samuel did not come to Gilgal; and the people were scattered from him. So Saul said, 'Bring a burnt offering and peace offerings here to me.' And he offered the burnt offering. Now it happened, as soon as he had finished presenting the burnt offering, that Samuel came; and Saul went out to meet him, that he might greet him. And Samuel said, 'What have you done?' Saul said, 'When I saw that the people were scattered from me, and that you did not come within the days appointed, and that the Philistines gathered together at Michmash, then I said, 'The Philistines will now come down on me at Gilgal, and I have not made supplication to the Lord.' Therefore I felt compelled, and offered a burnt offering.' And Samuel said to Saul, 'You have done foolishly. You have not kept the commandment of the Lord your God, which He commanded you. For now the Lord would have established your kingdom over Israel forever. But now your kingdom shall not continue. The Lord has sought for Himself a man after His own heart, and the Lord has commanded him to be commander over His people, because you have not kept what the Lord commanded you.'"*

Saul built his own table and it cost him everything. He tried to be righteous without the voice of God. In the old testament, the prophet is a symbol of the voice of God. Saul chose to build his own table of sacrifice and offering without the prophet. When the Prophet Samuel came, he told Saul that he built his own altar his own way and that is not the way of the Lord. The way of the Lord always is about communion, listening for His voice, but Saul, made it a powerless ritual. Unfortunately, this is the condition of many of our churches. They look righteous because they have the Bible present and an altar, but they do things their way without consulting the Lord at all. The Lord says this is not my church. My church walks in the power of My voice that drives away darkness.

## GIANT KILLERS GET KEYS FROM THE BROOK

*Luke 1:35-37, "And the angel answered and said to her, 'The Holy Spirit will come upon you, and the power of the Highest will over-shadow you; therefore, also, that Holy One who is to be born will be called the Son of God. Now indeed, Elizabeth your relative has also conceived a son in her old age; and this is now the sixth month for her who was called barren. For with God nothing will be impossible.'"* These are the words of the angel Gabriel to an innocent virgin named Mary who would be persecuted by her own people because of the miracle power she was called to carry and birth into the world. The problem with most modernized "Christians" (and I use this term loosely) is that they seek a more palatable message and lean toward consumerism which is the exact opposite of a true Christian walk. A true Christian walk is impossible for a person to accomplish alone  because it is by default, a call to carry something that is impossible for a man or woman to carry and birth without the continuous impartation of the Holy Spirit. All prophecy, dreams and visions follow this same pattern. If it's possible for a man or woman to do, it's biblical Kool-Aid. Only the Voice of God births life out of the darkness (John 1:1-5) and only the voice of God kills giants.

The contrast between Saul and David revealed who they really were when the giant came calling to rule over the nation of Israel. Saul, who lost the anointing of the Holy Spirit, acted like a king being present with the army, but he had no intention of facing the giant named Goliath. Saul listened to the voice of Goliath for forty days and did nothing but shake and tremble. But when David arrived on the scene, something inside of him that he learned to trust started burning in his heart saying, "Is there not a cause?" Saul was exposed as a fake, a Kool-Aid drinker, when the innocent boy named David, who trusted the voice of the Holy Spirit, was willing to run into a battle that was IMPOSSIBLE to win according to natural eyes. Saul quickly tried to take credit and tried to get David to wear his armor and make David look like he was under the "covering" of Saul.

*1 Samuel 17 38-40 "So Saul clothed David with his armor, and he put a bronze helmet on his head; he also clothed him with a coat of mail. David fastened his sword to his armor and tried to walk, for he had not tested them. And David said to Saul, 'I cannot walk with these, for I have not tested them.' So David took them off. Then he took his staff in his hand; and he chose for himself five smooth stones from the brook, and put them in a shepherd's bag, in a pouch which he had, and his sling was in his hand. And he drew near to the Philistine."*

Saul's armor is symbolic of a leader or person in charge who is afraid to do it themselves, never hearing the call because instead of communing with the One who rides a white horse, listening to His voice and executing His will, they instead choose to appear righteous and holy, building their own altar, but in reality they hide behind a Bible not really functioning in love with the Word of God, the Spirit of Prophecy. They don't know the One who speaks in the moment and gives golden keys, stones to the innocent to slay giants. They instead drink Kool-Aid and appear righteous to the masses until giant killers show up on the scene and expose them.

There are many "Sauls" using the context of "covering" to limit and control those who hear the Voice, trying to take credit as well as not be exposed as fake. The "Davids" who rely on the voice of God, running to the brook to get stones (keys) from the Holy Spirit need no "covering" from Saul. They have their covering, the voice of the Holy Spirit. These are the ones who shake households, cities, schools, regions and nations, unwilling to rely on Saul's armor (the fake system of religion) or drink his Kool-Aid. Instead giant killers run to the river of the Holy Spirit as they approach the battlefield of the world.

David was willing to run into the battle because he knew the Holy Spirit. Before David spoke to the giant, he stopped at the brook and pulled out five smooth stones. These five stones represent the grace of the Holy Spirit. It was with a stone from the brook that David killed the giant. The number five is the number representative of the grace of God. Grace is the very equipping of His Spirit who speaks and who is stronger than any force on earth. David had access to the Spirit of God and he relied on the voice of God only. The intent of Jesus sending the Holy Spirit after He conquered death, was to equip all of His sons and daughters as "David's" who would be trained by the Spirit to run to the brook and get weapons: prophecy, dreams, visions, words of knowledge, the working of miracles, faith, are all spiritual abilities that must be relied upon (1 Corinthian 12:4-11). They are the equipping of the Spirit. We will cover more on the gifts of the Spirit (the *Stones*) in a later chapter, but you must grasp the reality of how important this is as a means by which believers are expected to be victorious in the Spirit of God. Jesus said, *I will build my church and the gates of hell will not prevail – I will give you the keys (Matthew 16:13-19).*

The stones David received from the river of the Holy Spirit kill giants. The word you receive from the Holy Spirit has the same power as the stone David used to kill Goliath. But you must know, David refused any help from Saul because he recognized Saul could not help him. Actually, what Saul put upon him weighed him down. This is symbolic of churches who read the Bible but refuse the direct voice of God and the power gifts of the Holy Spirit. They look good, but when the giant arrives they shake on the mountain with Saul, afraid!

God raised up one son who would hear His voice and execute the vision. This one son named David not only killed a giant but awakened a dead nation who was not only under the spell of a giant, but a leader who served them Kool-aid with the Bible, appearing righteous but having no power! The witchcraft of the giant persisted for forty days without any hope of breaking out from under the spell until one young boy who knew the voice of the Holy Ghost arrived on the scene. When David went to the brook, he then turned to the giant and prophesied.

As soon as the words came out of David's mouth, the giant was a dead man. It wasn't David's words but the words of the One who rides the white horse wearing crowns and a robe dipped in blood with a sword in His mouth. The same Spirit of

Prophecy that came out in psalms and hymns when he was in the shadow of the wings of the ark and the presence of God was with him. David ate at the table with wine and bread where the rider of the white horse was positioned for battle and David knew he could not be defeated. He ran to the battle with a word of knowledge directly from the throne room of God and when David prophesied the vision, Goliath had no hope. The Lord Himself spoke through prophecy!

When David spoke to the giant the Word of the Lord, Goliath was a dead man.

*Samuel 17:45-47, "Then David said to the Philistine, 'You come to me with a sword, with a spear, and with a javelin. But I come to you in the name of the Lord of hosts, the God of the armies of Israel, whom you have defied. This day the Lord will deliver you into my hand, and I will strike you and take your head from you. And this day I will give the carcasses of the camp of the Philistines to the birds of the air and the wild beasts of the earth, that all the earth may know that there is a God in Israel. Then all this assembly shall know that the Lord does not save with sword and spear; for the battle is the Lord's, and He will give you into our hands.'"*

The words of verse 47 identify the battle plan of every believer. Run to the river of the Spirit, pray until He speaks, and then prophesy what He says.

This exposed Saul as a fake Kool-Aid drinker! Saul sought to kill David. Make no mistake, Saul is a symbol of a leader of a dead church, powerless to the giants of the earth. But when the Holy Spirit comes and raises up a David from within a dead house, the anointing on David will always expose the powerless, dead church. It doesn't matter how many Bible study meetings they have attended. When a son or daughter is anointed in the

Holy Ghost and called to do supernatural things, nothing can stop them.

If Kool-Aid drinkers are present in the midst of a David, there will be a war and they will try to hunt down the ones who follow the leading of the voice because the voice of the Spirit of God exposes the fake. When this contrast between the living and the dead is brought onto the scene, the fake will always function in its nature (hate, anger, bitterness, resentment). No matter how hard a person tries to "do what the Bible says," the Bible alone will never produce life because words on a page were never the final intent of God. The reason that philosophies (doctrines) separate people is because doctrines were never to be the center-piece of people gathering in organizations. You were not gathered to worship your interpretation of the Bible. People are to be centered on the Holy Spirit.

*2 Corinthians 3:17-18, "Now the Lord is the Spirit; and where the Spirit of the Lord is, there is liberty. But we all, with unveiled face, beholding as in a mirror the glory of the Lord, are being transformed into the same image from glory to glory, just as by the Spirit of the Lord!"*

Although the Bible is 100% true, each person must realize they have a destiny that can only be revealed by the Holy Spirit. Studying the scriptures must be relegated as a learning aid which is subject to the Holy Spirit, revealing to each individual in the right place, right time and for the right purpose. The Bible itself was never meant to be worshipped. In fact, the Law of Moses was designed to entomb a person because the Law of Moses does not have the power to cleanse the conscious and bring new life, but it only identifies the presence of sin (Hebrews 10:2). Jesus came as a man and went to the cross, symbolizing the entombing of sin and death. Jesus had to depend on the Holy Spirit even unto death. Jesus then, fulfilling the Law of Moses and all prophecies spoken of His coming, as well as the Revelation of John (Book of Revelation), were fulfilled in the resurrection.

*Matthew 5:17, "Do not think that I came to destroy the Law or the Prophets. I did not come to destroy but to fulfill."*

In Christ are all things and the Spirit of God goes on to explain in *Romans 6:3-6, "Or do you not know that as many of us as were baptized into Christ Jesus were baptized into His death? Therefore we were buried with Him through baptism into death, that just as Christ was raised from the dead by the glory of the Father, even so we also should walk in newness of life. For if we have been united together in the likeness of His death, certainly we also shall be in the likeness of His resurrection."*

The greatest revelation of the new testament is this: just as Jesus had to depend on the Holy Spirit for resurrection, so does every believer in Christ. A person who is Holy Spirit dependent becomes like David. God declared the Salt Covenant with David and the coming Messiah and all the promises of that Salt Covenant including the making of Giant Killers, rests on the shoulder of the Messiah, the Key of David.

# 9

# THE WEAPONS OF THE REDEEMER'S ARMY

## STONES FROM THE BROOK

1 Corinthians 14:1 "Pursue love, and desire spiritual gifts, but especially that you may prophesy."

IN 2017 I WAS IN A SMALL VILLAGE IN THE SOUTHERN COAST OF India. There was a small church of about 30 believers who had been calling my contact and asking us to come for several months prior to my mission. The mission was sixteen days and we had a two-day break between day 7 and day 9 that was not scheduled, so we decided to go to this remote place in India after we both had an unction of the Holy Spirit. To the natural eye, you would question why anybody would get on a plane when you could take a break in between the crusades and rest, especially if it only involved 30 people. Why would anybody get on a plane for 30 people? However, the Holy Spirit does not look at numbers. He finds people to do things based on what He says, not whether it is rational. Rational thinking is the enemy of those born of the Holy Spirit (Romans 8:6).

So, we boarded a plane and arrived late one evening with the intent of doing a meeting during the day and then an outreach type of crusade in the evening if we could gather enough people.

We woke up and were taken from the hotel to a small building. To our surprise, there were 52 teens and young adults in the room. All of them were Hindus. The 30 Christians who asked us to come remained outside praying so that the small room could hold all the young people inside. Before we started, one of the few Christian women who was working with the team to coordinate our meeting, said she was awakened that morning by a dream. She said an angel instructed her to go through the village from door to door and gather people for the meeting. She said she started early that morning knocking on doors so by the time we arrived they were waiting for us.

We began to introduce them to Jesus and the Holy Spirit and quickly started praying for them. A supernatural presence of the Lord Jesus came into the room and all 52 of these young people pledged their hearts to Christ and were baptized in the power of the Holy Spirit. The baptisms of the Holy Spirit started happening when a teenage girl experienced deliverance and many demons were cast out of her. As soon as this happened, all the young people started to weep, shake and experience deliverance. They all started to pray in tongues and a supernatural voice of the Spirit began to speak to these young people. They were all having visions of Christ and personal encounters with the Holy Spirit. We started bringing them up front one-by-one and they started telling the group what they were experiencing in the Spirit. Many had visions of angels coming to remove the darkness from their hearts and heavenly visitations from Jesus

Christ and the Holy Spirit. These visions resulted in deliverance and healing for many in the room. We had youth who started to prophesy what they were seeing in visions and there was a full-blown activation of the gifts of the Holy Spirit.

One of the youngest people in the room was a 13-year-old boy who had such a powerful encounter with the Holy Spirit that day that he was taken to heaven while he lay on the floor for over an hour that afternoon. When he got up off the floor, he started sharing that he was taken to heaven where Jesus took him into a room and equipped him with the clothing of a doctor and was told to come back and tell the people that Jesus heals. When he shared this with the group, there were people in the room who received physical healings. This meeting, which was to last for a few hours at most, turned into a full day of saturation in the Holy Spirit and people who would be changed forever. People gathered outside of the building and were looking at what was going on inside. It soon spilled out into the village.

When the meeting was over, these young people went back into their village and told many about what had happened. This resulted in over 1,000 Hindu people from the entire Hindu village coming to the meeting that night. When we started, I gathered all the young people who experienced the power of the Holy Spirit that day and lined them up in front of the stage and instructed them about what I was going to do and how to lay hands on people and pray in tongues.

I brought the young boy, who Jesus equipped as a doctor in the Spirit that day, on stage with me. I introduced the people to Jesus and the Holy Spirit and then had the young boy tell the crowd about his personal encounter with Jesus and the Holy Spirit that afternoon. As he was finishing his description of the encounter with Christ describing how Jesus heals, we heard screaming coming from the crowd. A woman came running up to the stage. My interpreter jumped down off the stage to meet her. After a few seconds, he turned around smiling at me. He screamed "She came blind, but now she sees!" The crowd immediately rushed the stage area. I instructed the 52 youth that were lined in front of the stage to lay their hands on the people and pray in tongues. People were overcome by the personal contact of the Holy Spirit. The whole crowd was praying in tongues for over an hour. There were mutes able to speak, deaf able to hear, and blind able to see. We had people testify of tumors disappearing from their bodies and countless miracles happened that night.

I want to emphasize the point that I was just a vessel to help orchestrate the sequence of events that led up to over a thousand people being baptized in the Holy Spirit and praying in tongues. We answered the call to go, but **it was the Spirit speaking that shook an entire village.** The angelic visitation to the woman and her response to go do what the Spirit of God told her to do, knocking on doors and gathering 52 Hindu youth, is what produced supernatural transforming encounters for the village.

It was then, when the vision given to the young boy, who less than 24-hours earlier worshipped idols, released the power of heaven through the vision of the Lord, producing miracles, signs, wonders and a thousand people weeping and praying in tongues for hours. This is the power of prophecy, dreams and visions. This is the power of the "David's" who run to the brook to get stones that kill giants and turn entire Hindu worshipping villages into those who will testify that Jesus Christ is alive and the one true God!

## TONGUES OF FIRE AND PROPHECY THAT OPENS PRISON DOORS

The point that the Holy Spirit is trying to establish in 1 Corinthians 14, is that tongues is the avenue by which you position yourself to hear the voice of God through visions, dreams and personal encounters with the Holy Spirit. Tongues will result in hearing and seeing in the Spirit. This is His voice. It is fresh bread for the spiritually starving children of the earth (Matthew 15:24-28).

His voice heard directly produces life (causes the darkness to flee). Those who have visions and dreams hear directly from the Holy Spirit and when the vision is prophesied to the people, the power of heaven is released to the people. Without the living manna from heaven, including prophecy and the gifts of the Spirit, the children of God starve (Matthew 15:22-29). Paul establishes prophecy as the power that brings deliverance, healing and personal introduction to the living God.

*1 Corinthians 14:24-25, "But if all prophesy, and an unbeliever or an uninformed person comes in, he is convinced by all, he is convicted by all. and thus the secrets of his heart are revealed; and so, falling down on his face, he will worship God and report that God is truly among you."*

Paul is using the term *if all prophesy*, to describe the intended result of you knowing the Holy Spirit and praying in tongues. As we discussed in the previous chapters, praying in tongues causes the voice of God to flow like milk to a newborn baby. Visions, dreams and prophecy flow from the voice of the anointing, the gift of tongues. The ultimate design of the Spirit is that all Christians will know the voice of God.

## THE POWER OF THE DIRECT VOICE OF GOD

*Mark 9:1-7. "And He said to them, 'Assuredly, I say to you that there are some standing here who will not taste death till they see the kingdom of God present with power (dunamis).' Now after six days Jesus took Peter, James, and John, and led them up a high mountain apart by themselves; and He was transfigured before them. His clothes became shining, exceedingly white, like snow, such as no launderer on earth can whiten them. And Elijah appeared to them with Moses, and they were talking with Jesus. Then Peter answered and said to Jesus, 'Rabbi, it is good for us to be here; and let us make three tabernacles: one for You, one for Moses, and one for Elijah'— because he did not know what to say, for they were greatly afraid. And a cloud came and overshadowed them; and a voice came out of the cloud, saying, **This is My beloved Son. Hear Him!**"*

Jesus declares to His three closest disciples that they will see the kingdom of God come in *dunamis* power (soul transforming power). When Jesus took them up the mountain, it was symbolic of the people being offered to come meet God face-to-face which was the original invitation to the Israelites when they were delivered out of slavery from Egypt (Genesis 20). However, they refused the invitation resulting in dead rituals through the law of Moses that could not save them. When Jesus came, the heart of David was the goal, equipping men to thirst for God the way God thirsts for sons and daughters.

When Jesus led them up the mountain, the very thing the people refused in the old covenant, Jesus foreshadowed being the Door that positions men to encounter the supernatural power of the Spirit. God the Father came to meet sons and daughters face to face. This is symbolic of childlike innocence coming transparent before the Father in the highest place (symbolic of spiritual prayer). Jesus walked them up the mountain physically and then He was transformed spiritually before their eyes. I believe what happened is the presence of God opened the spiritual eyes of their hearts to see Jesus as He really is, the One who goes forth conquering, the true WORD of God (Revelation 19:11-15). This is the power of entering the realm of glory where the Father dwells which accessible only through Christ. The Pharisees and Sadducees were very much like Adam in the garden after the great deception. When the Father came calling for His son, Adam hid, covering himself with fig leaves. Self-awareness drove them to hide. They were no longer transparent before the Lord (Genesis 3:8-11). They were no longer covered in glory as the fruit of the tree of knowledge of good and evil produced an orphan mentality.

In contrast, when Jesus, Peter, James and John stood at the very top of the mountain, the cloud came with the Father who spoke to His son transparently. They were all clothed in glory, no longer bound by earthly bodies, but adopted into the realm of glory. David dwelled in this glory becoming transparent before the Lord. In contrast the Pharisees and Sadducees covered themselves in the Law of Moses. The Law of Moses has a glory (2 Corinthians 3:12-18), but it is veiled (covered), unable to save.

All it has the power to do is point to the need of a savior. When the religious leaders covered themselves in the Law of Moses, they did the same thing Adam and Eve did in the garden. Instead of ascending the mountain, transparent before the Father, they covered themselves with words on paper. They made fig leaves out of the Bible. They remained orphans, appearing righteous on the outside, but darkened by what they covered themselves with on the inside. Their self-reliance kept them orphans.

But for those who ascend the mountain, coming transparent before the Father, adoption is the greatest gift. The power of adoption begins the building process; the unveiling process; of every person that ascends that mountain through the Spirit of adoption. When a person becomes transparent, the glory (destiny) of each son and daughter that was locked on the inside by the false coverings of self-reliance (shame), is unveiled through the direct voice of the Father. The new transparent relationship is anchored by the living voice of God who will always call forth each born-again believer into their true heavenly identity.

In Mark 9:7, the cloud overshadowed them, meaning the atmosphere was changed by the coming of the voice of God – the presence of God. The Greek word used to describe the Father speaking is the word *lego* which means to reorder, restructure, or establish the correct order. The *lego* power of the Father's voice transfigured them to *see* in the realm of the Spirit. The encounter is symbolic of what the Spirit of Prophecy releases into the atmosphere and the souls of men who are subject to the vision of the Lord.

Through the *dunamis* power of the kingdom, the presence of the living God, the Father who comes on a cloud to overshadow the people, speaks and establishes the kingdom of heaven in the hearts of men, putting the souls of the people in proper kingdom order by opening their spiritual eyes. The eyes of their heart! Like the young boy in the Hindu village whose spiritual eyes were open to see the living Christ as the Healer in heaven, and then testifying of seeing the living Christ, resulting in the Hindu people in the crowd being transfigured before our natural eyes! Sons and daughters are called to dwell in this glory and speak of the encounters with the Father, Son and Holy Spirit, which releases the realms of the Father's glory on earth!

## THE FORTITUDE OF PROPHECY, THE TRUE MERCY
## OF GOD

The Holy Spirit establishes a pathway for prophecy. *1 Corinthians 14:1, Pursue love, and desire spiritual gifts, but especially that you may prophesy.* The word *love* is the Greek word ***agape*** which means a love that is not of this world. It is supernatural love that releases supernatural power. Paul is saying to pursue Christ to such a degree that love is imparted continuously through heart to heart communion at His table. This supernatural love from Him will release supernatural abilities in the Spirit which equip you to love supernaturally. The result will be that you prophesy and change the world! Prophecy is a sign of a mature relationship built on hearing the voice of the Holy Spirit. The vision of the Lord always reveals the true destiny for people through His heart of mercy.

True love is transforming, resurrecting, life changing for all those in the hearing of the vision of the Holy Spirit. Jesus declared as soon as He was baptized in the Holy Spirit the Spirit was upon Him in *Luke 4:18-19, The Spirit of the Lord is upon Me, because He has anointed Me to preach the gospel to the poor; He has sent Me to heal the brokenhearted, to proclaim liberty to the captives and recovery of sight to the blind, to set at liberty those who are oppressed; To proclaim the acceptable year of the Lord.*

The love of Jesus Christ and the Holy Spirit releases transforming love that does things to heal, deliver, cast out devils and baptize, transforming the souls of men and women everywhere the Spirit of God is carried.

The redeemed truly know the mercies of God and that salvation is a gift, not an act of one's own decision to conform to the Ten Commandments. David's understanding of mercy is the deepest relationship expressed in the Bible, outside of Jesus Christ. As we discussed in previous chapters, David dwelt in the secret place of the Most High, under the shadow of His presence. This thirst for the Lord manifested in a love so deep that the Savior of the world would come as the Son of David having the authority of David upon His shoulder (Isaiah 22:22, Revelation 3:7). David declared in *Psalm 27:4, One thing I have asked of the Lord, and that I will seek: That I may dwell in the house of the Lord (in His presence) all the days of my life.*

David's heart was set on the presence of the Lord and the Lord responded by speaking to him and sharing the secrets of His heart. The psalms and prophecies came out of Zion because of David's heart burning in love with God. Jesus could have prayed for many things, but He prayed one thing for the disciples before He was crucified. *John 17:21, He said "I pray that they would be one with you Father just as we were One in Spirit" (PARA).* This connection with the Holy Spirit is love (supernatural agape love) which is the true source of spiritual gifts and prophecy. Paul's explanation of love in 1 Corinthians 13 is identifying love as the centerpiece of a relationship with the Holy Spirit and true prophecy will flow out of this love as the Spirit shares the heart of God to the one who hears Him.

The one who is in love and hears/sees His heart becomes the true prophetic voice of the Spirit sent to bring the mercies of God to the people. It is the mercy of God that delivers men who do not deserve salvation. According to the Law of Moses, the Hindu idol worshipers did not deserve salvation, but the mercy of God whose blood was poured out by Christ washing away their sin, created opportunity for the outpouring of the Holy Spirit to an entire village, that they would know the mercies of God, fall on their faces and worship Him. This is what love does.

First it hears the call to *go*, and then it speaks mercies through prophecy, dreams and visions to those who don't deserve it. True prophecy and words of knowledge transform people in moments of time.

This mercy, which can only be imparted by the Holy Spirit, sees men not as they are (without Christ), being lost, broken, and worthy of hell. But rather the eyes of mercy can look through their transformed eyes to see what God sees. Idol worshippers, sodomites, murderers, and people bound in every other sin you can identify are actually prisoners of this world and need a deliverer to break them out of the prison. And those who speak prophecy, dreams and visions from the Spirit reach through the entombment of the body and soul and pull forward the vision of God, their true destiny of heaven!

When Jesus looks from heaven and sees the earth an utter mess with people being captives to greed, poverty, disease, slavery and every other form of brokenness caused by sin, He looks not as one who condemns, but as the One who came to save the world and destroy the works of darkness (John 3:16, 1 John 3:8). He came to awaken the *Davids* who are born in iniquity, not having a chance at life, yet through the depths of His love, His voice makes them giant killers and kings. *Isaiah 59:19-21, AMP When the enemy shall come in like a flood, the Spirit of the Lord will lift up a standard against him and put him to flight for He will come like a rushing stream which the breath of the Lord drives. He shall come as a Redeemer to Zion and to those in Jacob (Israel) who turn from transgression, says the Lord. As for Me, this is My covenant or league with them, says the Lord: My Spirit, Who is upon you and Who writes the law, the flowing river of the Spirit of God inwardly on the heart, and My words which I have put in your mouth shall not depart out of your mouth, or out of the mouths of your true, spiritual children, or out of the mouths of your children's children, says the Lord, from henceforth and forever.*

## HEARING THE CALL TO RAISE THOSE DEAD IN SPIRIT

Every person clothed in the Holy Spirit must realize the world is a graveyard. It is a place bound to the law of sin and death. But the law of the Spirit (the flowing river of the Holy Spirit) continually flows, making us free from sin and death through the continual relationship with life (Romans 8:2). We were transformed on the mountain with Jesus, being transfigured ourselves and able to see spiritually, the will of God for the people. Having the gift of prophecy is equivalent to Ezekiel being led into the valley of death and being told to raise the dead. You have been resurrected in the Spirit in the midst of a graveyard and this same command is to you:

*Ezekiel 37:1-10, (AMP) "The hand of the Lord was upon me, and He brought me out in the Spirit of the Lord and set me down in the middle of the valley; and it was full of bones. He caused me to pass all around them, and behold, there were very many human bones in the open valley; and lo, they were very dry. And He said to me, 'Son of man, can these bones live?' And I answered, 'O Lord God, You know.' Again He said to me, 'Prophesy to these bones and say to them, 'O dry bones, hear the word of the Lord.' Thus says the Lord God to these bones, 'Behold, I will make breath enter you so that you may come to life. I will put sinews on you, make flesh grow back on you, cover you with skin, and I will put breath in you so that you may come alive; and you will know that I am the Lord.' So I prophesied as I was commanded; and as I prophesied, there was a thundering noise, and behold, a rattling; and the bones came together, bone to bone. And I looked, and behold, there were sinews on the bones, and flesh grew and skin covered them; but there was no breath in them. Then He said to me, 'Prophesy to the breath, son of man, and say to the breath, Thus says the Lord God, Come from the four winds, O breath, and breathe on these slain, that they may live.' So I prophesied as He commanded me, and the breath came into them, and they came to life and stood up on their feet, an exceedingly great army."*

## CALL THEM TO LIFE!

During my first few missions to India, I discovered that over 90% of the churches did not know the Holy Spirit or were even aware of the gifts of the Holy Spirit. I would tailor messages around the perceived needs of a church, trying to teach biblical principles. In addition, I became aware that the Hindu do not deny Jesus. They just think of Jesus as another one of their gods. The churches were full of people that were still practicing Hinduism with the outward signs of the Hindu religion.

During my first mission, Jesus came to me in a dream prior to a pastors conference and reordered my objectives. In this dream, Jesus walked with me through the front door of the hotel where some of the pastors were staying for the conference. Jesus took me to the first floor and opened the door to one of the rooms. He walked me over to the bed where there was a dead man laying on the bed. It was a pastor with a Bible in his hands. Jesus asked me a question: *Can these bones live?* I answered *yes Lord* and started prophesying to the man and life came into him. The man sat up alive. Jesus then took me into another room where another dead pastor was laying on the bed. He asked the same question; *Can these bones live?* I answered *yes* and started prophesying to the man and life came into him. The man sat up alive. Jesus then turned to me and spoke the same thing He said in the dream when He originally called me to India. He said, *Raise the dead, heal the sick, cast out devils and baptize in the Holy Spirit.*

Jesus was telling me that the pastors were not spiritually alive. They needed to be awakened from the dead by the power of the Holy Spirit. From that moment on, my mission became even more simplified. I have been in hundreds of churches in India and when we go in, very few know the power of the Holy Spirit. When we leave, they all pray in tongues. The pastors are then organized in multi-day meetings to teach them the gifts of the Holy Spirit and hearing the voice of God to equip the church in prophecy. We have established our ministry in India and have ministered to thousands of pastors who have been baptized in the Holy Spirit and expecting miracles signs and wonders everywhere they go. Eastern India is being resurrected! An army is being awakened!

# 10

# THE RIGHT PURPOSE AT THE RIGHT TIME IN THE RIGHT PLACE

## THE ROD OF AUTHORITY

Isaiah 11:1-2 There shall come forth a Rod from the stem of Jesse, and a Branch shall grow out of his roots. The Spirit of the Lord shall rest upon Him, The Spirit of wisdom and understanding, the Spirit of counsel and light, the Spirit of knowledge and of the fear of the Lord.

THIS PROPHECY IN ISAIAH 11:1-2 OF THE COMING OF THE MESSIAH reveals the full ability of the Spirit of God granted to Jesus Christ. This authority that Jesus Christ walked in was not simply an endowment with the freedom to go do whatever He wanted to do. True heavenly authority manifests through three keys including the equipping of the Spirit, a mind connected continually to the Spirit, and finally a heart that has the same mind of God. Jesus didn't function simply by what He was given. When Jesus went to the Jordan River and was baptized in the Holy

Spirit and the dove came upon Him from heaven (Matthew 3:16), Jesus demonstrated the "rod" that was prophesied in Isaiah 11:1.

A rod is a prophetic symbol of authority. The authority manifested by Jesus was not simply based on who He was, but hearing the voice of God and executing the will of God. Faith comes from hearing the voice of God and then executing the command. Self-willed acts, no matter how righteous they appear, are dust in the wind and will not produce fruit. Faith is a spiritual impartation of the Holy Spirit (Romans 10:17).

Authority, in this same manner, is released into the situation by people in the right place, at the right time for the right purpose. Everywhere Jesus went, the authority of heaven dominated the environment. It was not a biblical principle that fed the 5,000, delivered the demoniac who was chained to the tombs, awakened the woman at the well, or raised Lazarus from the dead. It was Jesus being in the right place, at the right time, with the right purpose. Jesus didn't function from a biblical principle. As we discussed previously, Jesus dwelled in prayer and came out of prayer with a battle plan given to Him by the Spirit. This battle plan is the will of God, and when executed, releases heaven on earth.

Authority has multiple dimensions and is not simply a God given right to a believer, but the manifestation of the power of heaven when you do what He tells you to do. For example, Jesus commanded us to go into the world and preach the gospel (Matthew 28:19). This is a conceptual authorization revealing that you have a calling and that He will be with you in that calling. However, the place, the time and the purpose are revealed only through His voice authorizing you in the right time, right place, with the right message. The relationship with the Spirit of God is designed to be the centerpiece of the covenant, with scripture being referenced, not worshipped. Scripture, no matter how true, will never tell you the right place, at the right time and the right purpose. Only the Holy Spirit can reveal that to you (Romans 8:11-15).

Jesus said all authority has been given to me and He gives it to believers not simply through believing the scriptures, but when His voice is heard and acted upon, ability to rule that place is made known. Think of the baptism of the Spirit as the granting of access to the heart of God. The access to the heart of God must be so valued that you become sensitive to your heavenly position through this access. Jesus said in *John 14:3, "And if I go and prepare a place for you, I will come again and receive you to Myself; that where I am, there you may be also."* The word **place** is the Greek word **topos** meaning *a position, or to occupy a place.* When you received the Holy Spirit through Christ (the Door), you are no longer bound as a man having a trapped spirit inside of a body. Instead, the door of Christ grants you access to heaven where your spirit can come boldly to the throne of grace through prayer and hear the voice of God (Hebrews 10:19-22).

Authority commands the spirit world through relationship in hearing His voice because the Spirit of God leads believers to the right place, at the right time with the right message. In Acts 19:13-17, the family of a Jewish exorcist saw Paul casting out devils in the name of Jesus so they decided to use the name of Jesus also. The story says that the demon beat the seven sons of this Jewish exorcist. The reason they were beaten is because authority is not simply a function of using the name of Jesus.

Authority is a function that flows from Him. His voice positions believers to be in the right place, at the right time, for the right purpose. In contrast, Paul casts out demons in Acts 19 under the full authority of Christ because Paul was sent to

Ephesus by the Spirit of God. The Spirit of God then led the sequence of events starting with believers of Jesus who did not have the power of the Spirit (Acts 19:1-6), then going into the synagogues for several years to break the dead religious traditions of the Jews contrasting the way of the Holy Spirit through Christ. Then, at the right moment, following the demonstration of the Spirit in casting out devils through Paul, the city brought their books of idolatry and witchcraft, burning them, launching a revival and the church in Ephesus (Acts 19:18-40). It wasn't Paul's work that started the revival, it was Paul hearing the Spirit and being in the right place, at the right time, for the right purpose, making a way through submission to the Spirit so that the Holy Spirit came upon the people. Paul became a door of the Spirit to the people. This is true authority.

The story I discussed in a previous chapter about the command I heard to go to Panera at lunch time was a major lesson in the authority manifest by hearing the Spirit and being in the right place, at the right time, for the right purpose. The Holy Ghost told me the time and place, and when I went, He revealed by vision, the intent of the Spirit. Obedience to the Spirit is what opened a door for the glory of God to come upon, not only the young lady in Panera, but all of the students back at her dorm room and the decision of these people to chase the Holy Spirit from that day forward. This was the will of God, not my will! I learned that day how great the contrast was between church goers spending their whole lives learning biblical principles versus the voice of God and being led by the Holy Spirit. The letter kills (in many ways), but the Spirit gives life (2 Corinthians 3:6)! Especially when you have twisted doctrines that relegate the Holy Spirit as an option to Jesus, instead of being the centerpiece of you truly functioning as a born-again believer having ACCESS to all authority through the realm of the Holy Spirit.

## THE SEVENFOLD SPIRIT OF GOD

The greatest deception still functioning in the church is people trying to live righteously, but still functioning from a religious operating system. Religious operating systems are based on biblical truths, but are subject to the will of man in determining when, where and how they want to apply the principles.

In contrast, is a Spirit-led life as the Bible commands, one lived through Christ, accessing His thoughts (Philippians 1:21; 2:5-8). There is no alternative other than personally knowing Him that produces life in you and the people around you. The only way you can execute in this fashion is to step out of the old religious thought process and give your mind to the voice of the Spirit (Romans 8:1-12). Satan's game plan is pretty simple. He first will work to keep you a slave to the world through a false identity. If somehow by the grace of God you do receive Christ as Lord, then his next great deception is to keep you a powerless Christian who just goes to church willing to perform religious rituals and doctrines, not knowing the Holy Spirit.

Satan's greatest fear is a person who knows who and what they are in Christ, because a person who knows who and what they are in Christ, will hear the voice of God and be in the right place, at the right time, for the right purpose. This happens through a prayer life with the Holy Spirit who pours out dreams and visions (Joel 2:28, Acts 2, Acts 10:17). Sons of God are born of the Spirit and they rely on the Spirit of God for life in the same manner in which Jesus walked on earth, clothed in the sevenfold

Spirit of God which Jesus promised to give to all who wait upon the Spirit of God (Luke 24:49).

## COUNSEL, WISDOM AND KNOWLEDGE REVEALED BY THE GIFT OF TONGUES

*Isaiah 11:1-2, "There shall come forth a Rod from the stem of Jesse, and a Branch shall grow out of His roots. The Spirit of the Lord shall rest upon Him, The Spirit of wisdom and understanding, the Spirit of counsel and understanding, the Spirit of knowledge and of the fear of the Lord."* I would like to emphasize that although there are seven spirits referenced, that *understanding* is a function of receiving *counsel, might* is a function of receiving *wisdom,* and the *fear of the Lord* is a function of receiving *supernatural knowledge* (*yada*).

Your relationship with the Holy Spirit will eventually reveal interactions with the Spirit of *counsel,* resulting in *might* being manifested in your life, with the Spirit of *wisdom* causing *understanding* to manifest in your life, and the Spirit of *knowledge* which will release the *fear of the Lord* into your life. When you receive the Holy Spirit, your encounters with the Spirit of God should increase over time, eventually making the Spirit world so much more real to you than the natural world.

This expansion into the realm of the Holy Spirit will grow as your dependence on the Holy Spirit grows. Daily prayer, alone with the Holy Spirit, praying in tongues, will produce greater and greater interaction resulting in the growth of your Spirit man. Think of tongues as the way of drinking the nourishing milk of the Spirit which will produce growth through visions and dreams, which will produce faith.

Faith only comes from hearing the voice of God. Faith

cannot be generated by the will of man. There are different levels of faith in the kingdom of heaven (Romans 12:3), but no matter where you are at today in your faith, I am here to tell you that faith grows like a seed. Faith is a spiritual gifting (1 Corinthians 12:4-11) and that gifting grows and works through love (Galatians 5:6). As you grow in your love for the Spirit of God, dwelling in the presence of the Most High, the voice of God not only speaks *to you*, but *through you*.

In recognizing that faith grows and is supernatural, something man cannot create, the source of faith must be so deeply understood and valued that your life becomes centered on the source of life, the Spirit of God. Your life and the ability to enter your calling is dependent upon your desperation for the Spirit to speak to you. The Holy Spirit is the ONLY connecting power of the new covenant. As the old covenant was connected through the words on stone (the Law of Moses), the new covenant is life giving, being connected through the voice of the Spirit. Yes, God speaks, and His intention is that faith grows in your life through this relationship of hearing His voice. As discussed previously, faith comes by hearing, and hearing by the **rhema** word (the direct spoke words of God) that imparts supernatural power to the hearts of sons and daughters of God (Romans 10:17).

I want to emphasize that Jesus didn't just send the Holy Spirit so that the gifts of the Spirit would simply be available. He actually is the *Door* that opens up the enclosure where the sheep are confined. Jesus said *"I am the Door"* John 10:7-10 *"Then Jesus said to them again, 'Most assuredly, I say to you, I am the door of the sheep. All who ever came before Me are thieves and robbers, but the sheep did not hear them. I am the door. If anyone enters by Me, he will be saved, and will go in and out and find pasture. The thief does not come except to steal, and to kill, and to destroy. I have come that they may have life, and that they may have it more abundantly.'"*

Most "Christian" theology is limited from the perspective that they view the word "saved" in verse 9 as an *act* instead of what it is really is intended to establish, which is continual access to heaven. Access to a place *(topos)*, a heavenly place in the Spirit prepared by Christ. As it stands, in this world you are locked in the realm of death, the earth, without Christ. However, Jesus is the *Door* that grants access to the realm of the Holy Spirit (heaven), not when your body dies, but when your soul is born again and enters the Spirit to dwell in the secret place of the Most High. That time is now. This is what a Christian prayer life is to be centered upon. You enter prayer to be embraced by the Spirit allowing the Spirit of God to lead you through dreams, visions and encounters in the realm of heaven. The Door (Jesus Christ) grants you access to continual counsel, wisdom and knowledge, and when your heart acts in alignment, you release understanding, might and the fear of the Lord upon the earth, just like Jesus (John 14:12)!

## LED BY THE SPIRIT

After Jesus sent me to India, Jesus began defining my work in specific areas with specific people, through a series of dreams and visions. In one particular dream, it started with me sitting on a chair in what appeared to be a waiting room. Across from me was a veil (curtain) that extended the length of the wall. There was a seven-branch candlestick in the room with me. There was nothing else in the room. The candlestick came alive with fire on every candle. It could bend fluently and it started to walk toward me. A face became visible on the main candlestick and it spoke to me saying, "The Counselor will see you now." The candlestick pulled back the veil and I entered.

I could see the Counselor standing with several angels pouring molten gold into a container that was roughly two feet square. As the gold began to harden, the Counselor asks me to step into the basin and bend over and touch the gold so that my handprints were in front of my footprints. I then I stepped out of the basin. When the gold was hardened with my handprints and footprints being visible, an angel came and broke it in half with my left hand and foot on one half and my right hand and foot on the other. The Counselor then picked up the seven-branch candlestick and placed the burning candle upon my tongue and wrote upon my tongue this scripture: *1 Corinthians 12:11, "All these things [the gifts, the achievements, the abilities the empowering] are inspired and brought to pass by one and the same Holy Spirit, Who apportions to each person individually, exactly as He chooses" (PARA).*

The Counselor then walked me over to a position on the floor where doors opened and I could see that it entered into the realm of the earth. There was another Spirit waiting for me at this door, his name was Wisdom. Wisdom took me by the hand and pulled me through these doors into the realm of the earth. Wisdom handed me two rods in which he placed each of my hands. The rods were the same, having a scripture written on each, Nehemiah 8:11. Two angels appeared and stretched my left leg and left arm to the USA, while my right leg and arm were stretched to India. I could see in both places the handprints and footprints that the Counselor made were already in these two nations. I was being stretched so that my hands and feet could be in the place that was destined for me to be.

The dream is now reality. Its meaning brought me to the

right place, with the right purpose, at the right time. The seven-branch candlestick is the Holy Spirit and the natures of Wisdom, Understanding, Counsel, Might, Knowledge and the Fear of the Lord which are all natures of Jesus Christ fully equipped by the Spirit (Isaiah 11:1-2). The Holy Spirit brought me through the veil (the wall of separation) to come boldly to the throne of grace (Ephesians 2:14; Hebrews 10:19).

The Holy Spirit opened the door to Counsel, which dwells in the heavenly realm, who equipped me with a burning fire to equip a specific people with the fire of the Holy Spirit. The Spirit of Counsel then opened the door to Wisdom whose job is to reveal understanding and strategy with the right people in the right place. Wisdom is who gave me authority (the rods) to impart the fire of the Holy Spirit to the masses in India having handed me the rods with the scripture of Nehemiah 8:11.

In Nehemiah 8, the masses of people were positioned in front of the Water Gate to hear the Word of God spoken for the first time meaning not just the words on paper, but the flow of the Spirit of God through the Water Gate. This is symbolic of the outpouring of the Holy Spirit, for the people to not only be granted the scriptures, but more importantly, the life granted by the Holy Spirit (the Water Gate). This is exactly what I do in India. The people are overcome by the Holy Ghost. Wisdom positioned me to meet the Spirit of Knowledge in specific cities in India where thousands of pastors, hundreds of churches, and hundreds of thousands of people have been baptized in the fire of the Holy Spirit. Again, this is what I do. This is my mission, and the connection point with America is focused on equipping specific churches in revival of the burning of the Holy Spirit, ultimately producing burning missionaries, revivalists and equippers of the fire of the Holy Spirit to go to the places and nations they are called to go.

## HIS WAYS ARE NOT OUR WAYS

I included this chapter to illustrate the importance of purpose, time and place. There is a part of my heart that still desires to be back in the church that I was in ten years ago in America where I led small groups and deliverance ministry. I loved it. I laughed and cried with the people, helping them in any way I could. We were being birthed in the Spirit together. I loved to spend hours with one person casting out many devils and prophesying, seeing that person be free and have a life that was visibly different. I was embedded deep in a church community.

However, the Holy Spirit had different plans. A call that required me to go to the place He called me to go. That place required that my comfort zone and place of protection be shifted in a manner that He would get the credit for what He was calling me to do. I had to learn to trust in a more supernatural way even though I was using the gifts of the Spirit in the church. There is a time when only He can teach you and prepare you to do an impossible thing. If I would have stayed in that single church, I never would have seen India like I have, let alone the thousands upon thousands of people who have been touched by the Holy Spirit in that nation.

His voice will often times require you to pick up your cross and follow, leaving safe places and relationships that somehow have taken part of your heart that is supposed to be His. His plans are beyond what we can even imagine. He often only lets us see part of the story, having to trust in the unknown. At the end of the day, the single thing that produces in the kingdom is faith working through love which is manifest by His living voice. The Seed of life. There is no substitute for you dwelling in the secret place of the Most High where He reveals secrets to those who love Him.

# 11

# THE GOSPEL SPEAKS

## PROPHECY CHANGES REALITY

Revelation 19:10-11 "For the testimony of Jesus is the spirit of prophecy." Now I saw heaven opened, and behold, a white horse. And He who sat on him was called Faithful and True, and in righteousness He judges and makes war."

I WAS MINISTERING TO A SMALL GROUP OF TWENTY-FIVE PEOPLE and was moved by the Spirit to prophesy. I saw a vision of an angel coming into the room. The angel had a name written upon him. It was the angel named Love. The angel was carrying a vial of golden oil. Written on the vial was the word *deliverance.* I saw the angel walk into the room and pour the vial of oil over the people. As I was prophesying what I saw in the Spirit, oil appeared on my face and was running down my chin and neck. Yes, oil appeared on my face! The people saw it and even came up to me and touched the oil that came from heaven. As they touched the oil they would fall to the ground under the power of the Spirit. There was great deliverance, healing and spiritual awakening that night. The Gospel invaded the room. Vision was the invitation and when the vision was prophesied, the realm of the Spirit entered the earth through Christ, the doorway.

There are different levels of faith in the kingdom of heaven with the ultimate level of faith being so dependent upon the Holy Spirit that when the mind is given to the mind of Christ, heaven literally invades the earth. *Romans 12:1-2, "I beseech you therefore, brethren, by the mercies of God, that you present your bodies a living sacrifice, holy, acceptable to God, which is your reasonable service. And do not be conformed to this world, but be transformed by the renewing of your mind, that you may prove what is that good and acceptable and perfect will of God."*

The issue is not the current condition of the world and the problems it poses to you. The issue is being able to see in the Spirit realm because as we learned previously with the calling of Jeremiah, the Lord was only concerned with one thing, Jeremiah's ability and trust in the vision of the Lord.

Faith is received by grace. Unfortunately, a lot of what we see today in the church is not faith, but the will of man. Faith functions differently and is a product of hearing the voice of God (vision). So, when a believer, who hears the direct voice of God, walks into a room, a city, a church, or a foreign nation, the vision of the Lord is the reality the Holy Spirit wants to release on earth. *Revelation 5:5, "Then one of the elders said to me, 'Do not weep. Behold, the Lion of the tribe of Judah, the Root of David, has prevailed to open the scroll and to loose its seven seals.'"*

The seals upon the earth are the things such as time, place and energy. These laws of physics lock each of us in a time, a place and spiritual position or energy. Better known as a prison.

When Jesus conquered sin and death and took the keys of death and Hades (Revelation 1:18), He became the One who holds all the keys (all authority) over time, place and spiritual position or energy. When Isaiah prophesied of the coming Messiah who would hold the key of David (Isaiah 22:22), it was a prophecy of the authority Christ would obtain in the death and resurrection, but also a prophecy of the authority that would be restored to man through the Spirit of God. As sons and daughters who hear the voice (the keys) that breaks through doors and overcomes time, they release the presence (the *dunamis* energy) of the Holy Spirit when they prophesy the vision of the Lord (Matthew 28:19).

This is true faith, because faith is only received by the Spirit, by hearing Him speak by voice or by vision. True visions and dreams of the Holy Spirit always change position (spiritual imprisonment) and the natural state of man (body, soul and spirit). He never leaves you or the people around you the way He found you. He gives gifts to men. The vision from the heart of Christ restores you according to His vision of your place, time and energy. This establishes your heavenly purpose on earth, your destiny according to heaven rather than earth. This is His grace!

## WHAT IS THE GOSPEL?

Buckle your seatbelt! In order to do extreme miracles, signs and wonders through the Holy Spirit, you must have absolute dependence on the vision given by the Holy Spirit. Trust and dependence are verified in action. This does not mean simply going to church. This means that you center your life in spiritual prayer with the Holy Spirit and go and execute the vision He gives you because as He said to Jeremiah, "I am well able to perform the vision!" In the book of Acts, the original church did not have a New Testament Bible. They were actually living it and it would be later documented in what we call the New Testament.

Since the early church did not have New Testament scriptures, their whole existence was centered upon following the voice of the Holy Spirit. Paul goes on to document the many revelations of what was prophesied in the books of the prophets, the promise of the new covenant through the mirror of the Old Covenant, and many other revelations, but these writings were not the focus of Christianity. They were guidance for the church to function, but those who led revivals and worked miracles in the book of Acts were dependent upon the voice of the Holy Spirit. This might come as a shock, but they were not Bible centered. They worshipped and had a relationship with the living God.

Over the years as writings and interpretations were collected from the encounters of the apostles and prophets, Paul references these revelations as being good for training in the way of the Spirit and establishing spiritual doctrines, but they were never meant to be what is worshipped or become what the Pharisees and Sadducees made the writings of the Old Testament. We are ultimately to be trained in the doctrines but living in absolute trust of the living voice of God, relying solely on the voice of the Holy Spirit (Hebrews 6:1-4). Only the living God is to be worshipped, which is the way of David. David knew the Spirit so well that the prophecies and psalms that flowed out of David's heart in Zion are what ministered to him and the people around him.

This same Holy Spirit was poured out on the day of Pentecost to restore the Tent of David and establish the church as a church of intimacy and power. Intimacy and power are synonymous. They go hand-in-hand. True Holy Spirit power does not come without learning absolute trust and dependency on the voice of God. Unfortunately, instead of teaching the simplicity of the Holy Spirit, most of our churches and seminaries spend 90% of their time teaching and debating scripture, justifying their points of view. This is a major error in the modern church. We should be a witness of Christ through the power of the Holy Spirit and let Christ witness for Himself, in person, to a dying world in need of resurrection!

Revelations of the Spirit were written down and became great teaching doctrines for believers. Spiritual encounters such as Pater's vision of the sheet from heaven in Acts 11 or John's vision of the revelation of Christ are great for teaching and learning, but only the Spirit of God can truly teach you (Isaiah 28:9-11). The origin of these teaching doctrines was the Holy Spirit. Peter and John learned from vision, or better yet, they received impartation from the Spirit through visions. It was the encounter that imparted the supernatural including wisdom, understanding, counsel, might, knowledge and the fear of the Lord. They did not sit around centering their whole Christian existence on doctrinal positions, like many of today's Christian denominations and seminaries. They centered their life on the Holy Spirit and introducing people to the Holy Spirit. The church grew at astounding rates.

Paul states, *"Walk by faith, not by sight"* (2 Corinthians 5:7). Faith is not doctrine dependent. It's not *doctrine* that is capable of producing faith. Faith is imparted by the direct voice of God through the Holy Spirit and is undebatable. It is the ultimate witness of Christ Himself. The meaning of scripture can be debated endlessly. As a result, we have an endless number of denominations and splinter groups, who defend their interpretations of scripture more than they depend on the Holy Spirit. Denominations end up being doctrinally centered, and the people gather around what they perceive is truth. This results in continuous splintering of people groups because their theology drives their mission.

It gets twisted because all doctrinal error will drive dependence on the doctrine instead of the Teacher, the Holy Spirit. Jesus didn't send a book; He sent the Holy Spirit. He said that when He, the Spirit of Truth comes, He will guide you into all truth (John 16:13). Truth is a person who leads people into trust, dependence and action. Today, there is more time spent debating doctrines than introducing people to the Spirit of Truth. Maybe we are just functioning from the wrong definition of the gospel.

## THE SPIRIT OF PROPHECY TESTIFIES PERSONALLY TO THE HEART

*Galatians 3:8-9, And the Scripture, foreseeing that God would justify the Gentiles by faith, preached the gospel to Abraham beforehand, saying, "In you all the nations shall be blessed." So then those who are of faith are blessed with believing Abraham.*

Jesus Christ came and spoke directly to Abraham in visions and dreams and has documented the means of justification. He believed in the dream, the gospel revealed personally to him and he was accounted righteous. When the Spirit of Truth came to Abraham in dreams and visions, there was an impartation and introduction to the God of the universe to know God, to reveal destiny, and be with Abraham to lead him into promise. This connection to the Spirit of God and the following of the promise of the Spirit, produced righteousness through faith in the gospel that was preached to Him (Romans 4:1-4).

Paul references this relationship as producing righteousness and being the model of faith. The gospel speaks! As in my own personal testimony, I spent 20 years growing up in a denomination that trusted the love letter we call the Bible, but did not rely on the Holy Spirit, resulting in me seeing a powerless religion. However, when Jesus spoke to me directly the night I was baptized in the Holy Spirit (see the introduction), faith was imparted to me and the power of the Holy Spirit manifested when I prayed, prophesied and cast out devils.

The Bible is not a substitute for the direct voice of God. If you recognize this, you will understand the power of prophecy and the gifts of the Spirit. The gifts of the Spirit are the manifestation of the real gospel of Jesus Christ, presenting the living God to the people and not just the love letters of the Bible. I have seen people read the Bible for decades and nothing happens, but when the Spirit of Prophecy speaks through a man, I have seen the dead raised, the crippled walk, the blind see and the deaf hear, with entire congregations being baptized in the Holy Spirit. The Spirit of Prophecy is the light that invades the darkness in real-time.

The Spirit of Prophecy is a person, and my testimony is that when I prophesy through the visions he gives me, Jesus Himself is the witness. I am a carrier of His vision and when I speak the vision, Christ witnesses. He invades the earth as the Spirit of Prophecy when the vision is spoken. This is the testimony of knowing Him. You are a vessel pouring out oil that never runs dry. The promise of being with you (John 14:18), is absolutely true. When you introduce Him to people through prophecy and all of the gifts of the Spirit, you are literally introducing them to the person of Christ and the opportunity for real intimacy, not just love letters (scripture). The scripture is not the primary witness. The Spirit of Truth is the witness. I bring the Spirit of Truth everywhere I go and He is the One who works miracles, signs and wonders, reading the hearts of men, revealing their issues and destinies with words of knowledge and the result is that men fall to their knees and declare Jesus Christ is Lord. This is the witness of the living God!

## CHARIS-MANIACS

The word grace is the Greek word **charis**. *Charis is the root word Paul uses when he is explaining the gifts of the Holy Spirit. 1 Corinthians 12:4-11, There are diversities of gifts (Charisma), but the same Spirit. There are differences of ministries, but the same Lord. And there are diversities of activities, but it is the same God who works all in all. But the manifestation of the Spirit is given to each one for the profit of all: for to one is given the word of wisdom through the Spirit, to another the word of knowledge through the same Spirit, to another faith by the same Spirit, to another gifts of healing by the same Spirit, to another the working of miracles, to another prophecy, to another discerning of spirits, to another different kinds of tongues, to another the interpretation of tongues. But one and the same Spirit works all these things, distributing to each one individually as He wills.*

The best way I can explain the gifts of the Spirit being a function of grace is using the Greek language. The **charis** you receive from the Holy Spirit through visions and unction, is **charisma** (gifting of the Holy Spirit) to the people. You receive grace to give grace. The vision of the Holy Spirit builds the body. True grace is a function of a person giving their life in relationship to the Spirit of God, dwelling in the presence of God, and hearing the voice of God through visions, dreams and encounters. In turn, this is then prophesied to the people, bringing the power of heaven to earth, transforming lives with words of knowledge, faith and prophecy, giving sight to the blind, causing the deaf to hear, and the broken lifted up. This is grace!

When a person is willing to give their life to the Lord in prayer, willing to speak by the Holy Spirit, the people are transformed as a creation of the Holy Spirit, not a creation of doctrine. Doctrine has no power to create. In fact, doctrine oftentimes will limit the creative power of the Spirit because it erodes expectations when a person defaults to a perceived boundary. Scripture becomes a boundary that is oftentimes never crossed because it produces in a person a thought process that says, *I already know the answer.* When you already know the answer, you become a god instead of expecting in God.

In contrast, King David demonstrated expectation in the Spirit continually. His love for the presence of God and expectation of the Lord's continual deliverance made a way for God to continually CREATE in David's life. As an example, when David is made king, the Philistines immediately rallied to fight against him and challenge his new kingship. They did this twice within the first year of his reign as king, each time going to meet David and his army in the valley of Rephaim (the Valley of Giants). Prior to the first battle, David sought direction from the Lord. The Lord responded with instructions to go directly into the valley. David then acted as instructed and the Philistines were defeated.

Soon after, the Philistines rallied again and went to meet David in the same valley. David then portrayed his absolute dependence on the Holy Spirit instead of thinking in a routine fashion. David could have said that the Lord already spoke the first time and David could have just led his army directly into battle. However, David did not bypass expecting in the Lord to do a new thing. The Bible says that when David sought the Lord prior to the second battle, the Lord told him to wait adjacent to the mulberry trees, saying, *When you hear the marching sound of the angels in the trees, then advance onto the battlefield.* David did exactly as the Lord instructed and when he went out to battle the second time, it was essentially over before he stepped foot on the battlefield.

The Lord demonstrated providing two different paths of action in two different times, but at the same place, the Valley of Giants (2 Samuel 5:17-25). The lesson here is absolute, *Holy Spirit dependence.* David demonstrated how to wait and expect God to do a new thing through the power of the Holy Spirit in a manner that was completely different from the way God had moved before. This illustrates the difference between reliance on the Holy Spirit versus dead religious doctrines, which imprison people to do the same thing in the same place according to their own false expectations. We need Davids who are absolutely dependent upon the Holy Spirit to do a different supernatural thing every day of their lives, even if they remain in the same place battling the same thing. David's strength is that he *expected God in everything and assumed nothing based on previous experiences!*

## WILLINGNESS TO BE LED BY CHARISMA

Billy Graham was quoted as saying that if you took the Holy Spirit out of the churches, you would not be able to tell the difference in most churches because they look the same and do the same thing, never really expecting a move of the Holy Spirit. It is a sad fact today that even those churches that claim to be *Spirit filled* are organized in such a fashion as to schedule out any potential for the Holy Spirit to speak to the congregation in a moment's notice. What I mean by this is that even most Spirit filled churches become more responsive to the popular needs and wants of the people than the moving of the Holy Spirit. The leaders become like Saul and build their own altar of Kool-Aid, using the Bible as the thing that appears righteous, but they do not center the organization around the table of communion with the Spirit of Truth.

Therefore, the church services become routine and sequential, having no resurrection power. Everybody knows there will be 40 minutes of worship, 15 minutes of announcements and an emphasis on tithing, and then a message from the pastor, leaving no room for the Holy Spirit to speak in the moment and fight the battles that each person faces on that particular day. Most of which unfortunately is not the Gospel, even if they read the Bible. The true Gospel speaks, led by the most powerful force in the universe, introducing people to Jesus Christ, the conqueror, every time they gather. What is the purpose of gathering if the living God is not the voice leading the meeting? The Living Voice will always cause men to fall and be overcome by the Holy Spirit in resurrection power. My prayer is that everywhere I go, people would say that the living Christ, the Spirit of Prophecy who heals the brokenhearted, brings sight to the blind, opens prison doors, and brings deliverance to the captives, is with me. I fear being in front of Jesus one day and Him saying that I did not introduce Him to the people.

## THE STRATEGY OF YOUR ENEMY

Your enemy is strategic and purposed in one thing, dividing you from the anointing of the Holy Spirit. *1 John 2:18-19, Little children, it is the last hour; and as you have heard that the Antichrist is coming, even now many antichrists have come, by which we know that it is the last hour. They went out from us, but they were not of us; for if they had been of us, they would have continued with us; but they went out that they might be made manifest, that none of them were of us.*

The antichrist spirit is already here and it works most deceptively inside the church. Yes, that's right, its most deceptive work is inside of the church working to prevent, deceive, steal, dilute and devalue your encountering and dependence on the Holy Spirit. The word Christ is the Greek word *Christos* meaning covered in oil or smeared in oil, symbolizing the Holy Spirit. Jesus was fully clothed in the anointing, the Holy Spirit, hence Jesus the Christ. All authority occurred in the anointing of the Holy Spirit, hearing the voice of God continually.

It is interesting to note that the only time Jesus spent speaking scriptures was when He went to the synagogue to confront the Pharisees and Sadducees, turning over their money tables and confronting their lies, indicating they were the spawn of Satan who deceivingly used the Bible to control and manipulate people in dead doctrines. The modern-day church is not supposed to look like a synagogue where the majority of time is spent on Bible teaching. Bible teaching is necessary, but without the demonstration of the power of the Holy Spirit to heal the sick, cast out devils, baptize and even raise the dead, the churches, no matter how righteous or eloquent they look, reflect more of the synagogue than they do the book of Acts. We all are called to write our own supernatural story in the book of Acts. What is your Acts story?

## THE DREAM OF SATAN'S STRATEGY IN THE CHURCH

I was taken to hell in a dream where I saw the following. Jesus took me by the hand, leading me through the gates of hell. Jesus begins to point out that Satan's primary focus is on one section of hell where the title on the wall is *Angels of Light*. Satan is directing the work personally. As I am looking, it appears confusing because the demons appear as angels of light. They do not look evil to the natural eye. These angels of light are operating two factories. One factory prints Bibles. The other factory produces a liquid that appears pure white. The Holy Spirit picks up a vial of this white liquid, revealing the word *surfactant.*

I then see Satan coordinating teams of these angels of light and sends them to churches with the surfactant liquid and extra Bibles. Jesus and I then follow one of these teams out of hell and through the front door of a church. Inside the church I see people who are dripping with a golden oil. These teams of demonic angels surround certain people who are dripping with this golden oil and begin pouring surfactant over their head. The surfactant would dissolve the oil and cause their entire bodies to dry up with a sticky residue on their skin. The other demonic angels would then open the Bibles they brought with them and tear out pages and apply the pages to the body of the person who just had the oil removed by the surfactant. When these angels of light were finished, the people who were once dripping with the anointing oil were now dry and covered with pages of the Bible.

The demonic angels would then fit these people with harnesses and place heavy stacks of Bibles on them that were so heavy that the people could not stand. They would fall to the ground under this weight and unable to stand because the Bible pages, without the oil, became a burden. Jesus then turns me toward the pulpit to see why this was happening in the church. I see angels from heaven as well as these demonic angels (angels of light) surrounding the preacher. The angels of heaven are offering the anointing oil while the demonic angels are offering the surfactant (the antichrist spirit). The preacher mistakenly offers both to the people because he doesn't want to offend anybody and is not wholeheartedly sold out for the anointing oil. The subtle offering of both surfactant and anointing oil causes even those who received the anointing, to become dry and brittle because the surfactant begins to rub on people throughout the church, diluting the power of the anointing. Jesus turns to me saying, "Get the surfactant out of My Church!"

*Angel of light* is a term Paul used to describe Satan, or an agent of Satan, in 2 Corinthians 11:14. A surfactant is a chemical used to dilute oil or break oil apart. It is defined as an anti-oil agent, or a dissolver of oils. When oil tankers spill large amounts of oil in the ocean, they spray surfactant on the oil to dissolve it and break it apart so that the properties of the oil no longer exist. The Holy Spirit was showing me the surfactant as an illustration of the war against the anointing of the Holy Spirit. The surfactant is symbolic of the antichrist spirit sent into the world to deceive and destroy the full dependence upon the Holy Spirit. Anything that deceives a person from trusting the Holy Spirit could be said to be the antichrist spirit, especially doctrines that steal absolute dependence on the Holy Spirit.

I believe this is a crucial hour because there are many

pastors who are trying to build a church by subtly offering the Holy Spirit as an option, and because the Holy Spirit is not being presented as the only way to enter into Spiritual sonship (Romans 8:14), pastors and their congregations are being weighed down and enslaved by religion. Jesus' anger was vehement against the Pharisees (false Shepherds) who weighed down the people with conditions of the Bible, driving them to try and *achieve* the conditions of the scripture instead of introducing them to the Holy Spirit.

Instead of introducing people to the real teacher, the Holy Spirit, they weighed down the people with the burdens of the Law of Moses, sticking page after page of the Bible upon the people without the anointing. The letter kills, but the Spirit gives life (2 Corinthians 3:4-6). Jesus said to the Pharisees, *You are of your father the devil, you are dead men's bones and white-washed tombs.* The presence of scripture does not mean the people are alive in Christ. Only the anointing of the Holy Spirit raises the dead, opening their spirit man to the realm of the glory of God! Jesus died to send the promise of the Father (Luke 24:49) and destroy the work of the antichrist spirit (1 John 3:8).

Jesus is saying, *Get the antichrist spirit out of the church!*

# 12

# THE DESPERATE HEART OF DAVID

## MY HEART IS FOR MY BRIDE

Song of Solomon 5:8 "I charge you, O daughters of Jerusalem,
if you find my beloved, that you tell him I am lovesick!"

I HAD BEEN IN INDIA DURING ONE MISSION FOR OVER A WEEK AND
it was late in the afternoon when we entered our fifth church for
the day. I was exhausted and I still had several days of ministry
ahead of me. As we were driving to the church, for a moment I
thought, let's make this church quick and get out so I can get
back to the hotel and sleep for a few hours before the crusade
that night.

Suddenly, the Holy Spirit spoke to me saying, *There is a
woman with an issue of blood.* I had never preached before on the
woman with the issue of blood. When we arrived, I took the
congregation to the scripture about the woman with the issue of
blood and developed the context of story for a few minutes. A

few minutes into the story, the pastor's wife suddenly started crying so hard that tears were bouncing off the floor. She then laid face down on the floor and began to wail with such a desperate cry to God that all attention was upon her.

After a few minutes, she jumped up off the floor and ran into the back of the church out of site. A few women in the congregation went with her. The pastor of the church approached me and my interpreter as we stood in front of the church. We were in the midst of a supernatural moment of the Holy Spirit, but at the same time, it became strangely awkward as the pastor stood looking shocked and angered at the same time. He whispered a question to my interpreter, *did you tell him!?* The interpreter answered with a question, *tell him what?* The pastor said, *Did you tell him that my wife has been bleeding for over twenty years?* He was angry because he thought his wife was being tricked into thinking there was hope. They struggled for many years trying to preach Jesus to the Hindu people, but never experienced miracle power of the Holy Spirit.

At this moment, the congregation was aware of what was going on because they knew that the pastor's wife had major issues of bleeding and was near death on many occasions. They prayed for her for years, but to no avail. All of the people were standing at this point. I was concerned because although I received a word of knowledge from the Holy Spirit and it was confirmed with the reaction of the pastor's wife, I did not know how the situation could be turned around because the pastor was obviously uncomfortable and the crowd was focused on him, as well as looking to the back of the church for the pastor's wife. Just then, the pastor's wife and the other women came screaming back into the sanctuary. She was screaming, *I am healed, I am healed! There is no more bleeding! The bleeding has stopped!*

The people were ecstatic and so amazed that the whole congregation, who did not know the Holy Spirit, came forward to be touched like the pastor's wife. They ran to the altar, lovesick! The congregation was in the routine of coming to church, but on this day, they ran to altar desperate to be touched like the pastor's wife. They cried out like she did on the floor before the miracle. The bride was suddenly chasing Christ like He was chasing her. He revealed Himself as real and deeply in love with His bride, the church!

### ARE YOU AS LOVESICK FOR HIM AS HE IS FOR YOU?

In Song of Solomon chapter 5, the story of the romance between the king and the bride is described as the bride having known the king, but her sensitivity to his voice was non-responsive, or hesitant at best. The bride's heart was hardened to some degree as she sensed her beloved's presence from her bedroom, but she made excuses as she lay in bed, rationalizing why she would not get out of bed to answer the door and allow the king to come into the bedroom. She suddenly was convicted and ran to the door, but by the time she opened it, the king was no longer present. She was then awakened to His calling and she ran into the streets crying out for her beloved to return declaring, *If you see my beloved, tell him I am lovesick!*

How does a person respond when they think they are lovesick, but are really in a state of contentment or even just being numb? Not really in need, and definitely not desperate, being lukewarm is the most dangerous state of the heart. The bride can represent an individual, or a body such as the church (the Bride of Christ). The intent ultimately is a bride that is in desperate love with Him as much as He is for her. Desperation is the pinnacle of relationship and is the motive that fuels the power of love.

Without desperation, you just go through the motions. Life and all of its twists and turns, drains the energy out of most people. The world and its problems make it easy for even those who feel the tug on their heart, or have even experienced the depths of the Holy Spirit, to revert back to *normal life*. Like the bride of the beloved in Song of Solomon 5, instead of desperation for the king, most of our churches spend more time on things such as doctrines, defending their beliefs, hierarchy of leadership, submission, order, and finances, instead of being centered upon our King. These all take the place of being sensitive to His presence and desperate to the voice of His coming to the door of our hearts. This brings us to the question: What does desperation look like?

## SEEING REALITY

The Holy Spirit started waking me up in the middle of the night beginning in May of 2005, soon after the night I heard Him speak to me for the first time. My heart became sensitive to the presence of the Holy Spirit. It was not then, and is not now, unusual for my eyes to suddenly open, aware of the voice of the Holy Spirit talking to me about the Bible, the church, my family, and more often than not, the condition of my heart and His vision of deliverance for my life. But one night in December of 2012, He woke me up and spoke to me about my prayers for revival. I suddenly felt a sorrow in my spirit in a way that I never felt before, so I went to my office downstairs to continue our conversation and pray.

As soon as I sat in my chair, the Lord's voice thundered in the room. There was a tenseness in His voice that was different, more elevated and penetrating than normal. He asked me a question: *Is Laodicea in your church?* I paused because His voice was causing my heart to quiver, and I felt deep sorrow. Before I could make a sound, He answered His own question saying, *YES!* He then asked, *Do you know why?* Again, before I could answer, He answered His own question again, saying *Laodicea is in your church because Ephesus is in your church!* The root of all error, in all churches is when the church leaves their first love! What I felt that night was the reality of the heart of the King who gave everything for His church (His bride), and thirsts for a bride that would not lay content in her bedroom, but would be sensitive to His voice, sensitive to His coming presence in such a way that there is no other way to describe her heart condition, other than being flat out desperate. So lovesick that she would be waiting to pull Him into her bedroom!

The Lord let me feel His heart that night in a way that I had never experienced before. But little did I know, that was just the beginning of what He was doing to open my heart in recognizing my heart position, as well as the heart position of the church. The reality is that if you ask most pastors and leaders of churches if they are centered on Christ, they will answer *yes* and give you reasons based on all of the doctrines they believe and defend. They will list things like their efforts in the community, the way in which the church youth program is active, and the list goes on. Some will even promote the fact that they have great tithing rates, or even believe in the gifts of the Holy Spirit. However, the reality is that when you start pulling back the layers, you find out that many doctrines hold center stage over the simplicity of a heart in a desperate relationship with the Holy Spirit.

## WHAT DOES A DESPERATE BRIDE LOOK LIKE?

Needless to say, this one encounter with the Lord rocked my world. It started turning everything upside down. A few months later, Jesus encountered me in another way that shook me. He came to me in a dream. In the dream, He woke me up from my bed, and Jesus put His hand on my shoulder leading me downstairs to my office. He had me sit in my office chair and then took a sticky note and began writing on it. He stuck the note on my computer screen. I started to read it. It said, *Get to the place of desperation and I will visit you like I visited Jacob!* I was shocked. I turned to look at Him, but He was no longer present in the dream. I woke up and felt like I was in an absolute daze. What does He mean by, *get to the place of desperation?* I pray, I fast, and I minister to all kinds of people. What does He mean and how am I missing it? What are you leading me into Lord?

Soon after this encounter, I experienced a time, in the dark night like Jacob who said, *I'll not let you go until you bless me (Genesis 32:26)!* I found my prayer being different in this time of need. It wasn't like I was praying because I wanted to pray. I prayed because I *needed* to pray. The night was so dark, I couldn't leave go. This season of desperate supplication and praying in tongues until my body, soul and spirit were so saturated in His presence, was like a drug addiction. I became so needy of His presence that I prayed until I could not feel the pain in my heart.

After a year of learning desperate prayer and hunger for His presence, I learned there is a state of being where no religious

Christian doctrine, and no amount of doing anything biblical, other than *desperate prayer* could produce the connection with the heart of Christ that He so desperately desires of us. But why would the Holy Spirit do that to a man? Couldn't I have just learned about that in church or reading a book?

The next thing that happened was the Lord calling me to India. The missions were absolutely amazing! I saw thousands upon thousands of people baptized in the Holy Spirit and hundreds of miracles, signs and wonders. However, as supernatural as these several weeks would be, when I returned to the USA, I would experience a deep grieving in my heart. I would go into churches to minister and tell the stories, realizing there was a huge difference between the desperate need for a miracle in India versus congregations that *kind of wanted God, but were unwilling to beat down heaven's door to meet Him.* I was standing in front of people who have been lulled to sleep by a culture that provided stimulation for everything, but also numb to the King who stands at the threshold waiting for the response of the bride.

It was unexplainable how my heart felt. I would find myself weeping for no reason, and it intensified during my times of prayer because my questions centered on seeking revival for those dead in heart. *Why are you so real in India, Lord? Why do you reveal yourself so boldly and purposefully to the idol worshippers and those so bound in poverty to such a degree that words do no justice in trying to explain to the average American church goer how painful life is for the average person in India? How do so many idol worshippers literally run to the altar for prayer and suddenly begin praying in tongues and tangibly feel the love of God for the first time in their life? This does not fit the theology of even the majority of Spirit filled churches in America Lord!*

These periods of time back in the USA following the missions in India, were intense. I could suddenly see the living from the dead inside the church. It hurt because I could feel the pain in the Spirit, and I was angered because of the great deception of powerlessness and contentment in our churches. I realized the Holy Spirit was not really concerned about their idols in India because He could work with desperate hearts. He could deal with that very easily. It was the heart condition of desperation that opened the door for the Holy Spirit to invade their lives and reveal Himself so powerfully that they were changed forever. They were desperate for a savior, a deliverer, a hero! These supernatural encounters with thousands of Hindus getting so filled with the Spirit that they would weep and begin praying in tongues, crying out for the living God. These people who had no *Christian theology* watched me cast out demons and baptize people in the Holy Spirit and then they would simply give away what they were given.

People would be in a village in the days following the crusades and I saw them standing in the threshold of the door, praying for fellow Hindus on the street and they would end up baptizing people in the Holy Ghost. They simply gave away the grace, the power of the Holy Spirit which had been given to them just hours or days earlier. Watching this changed everything for me because I realized that instead of limiting the Holy Spirit by our doctrines and theologies and arguing about the right way of doing things, maybe we just need to get desperate for the Holy Spirit and in turn, give that desperation away because we simply stand in the threshold of that doorway where the Bridegroom said He would meet us. There is nothing like being so absolutely undone in the Holy Spirit that our hearts can see the contrast between being desperately expecting and needing the King versus the numbness of simply attending church meetings.

## TRUE UNITY AND A BRIDE WITH THE SAME HEART

Laodicea was the church that Christ said was lukewarm. *Revelation 3:16-18, So then, because you are lukewarm, and neither cold nor hot, I will vomit you out of My mouth. Because you say, 'I am rich, have become wealthy, and have need of nothing'—and do not know that you are wretched, miserable, poor, blind, and naked— I counsel you to buy from Me gold refined in the fire, that you may be rich; and white garments, that you may be clothed, that the shame of your nakedness may not be revealed; and anoint your eyes with eyesalve, that you may see.*

The Holy Spirit woke me up several years earlier, revealing that we were of the mindset that we were clothed in His presence, but in reality, we were naked and numb in heart. We thought we were on fire, but the Lord had a different view. He viewed the path we were on as lukewarm. The reason for this was that we left our *First Love*. We had all the lights and the great singers, a nice building and great seats. We had good speakers and we even had what you would call *moves of the Spirit*. However, we became more organized around the system, losing our simple hunger and thirst for His presence. We were not centered any longer on the Holy Spirit. We let the Holy Spirit have pieces of services, opening the door periodically in between our *other initiatives*. We even let the Holy Spirit minister in certain times through Spirit filled ministers, but as a group, doctrines and allegiance to the system became more important to the core leaders than the original hunger and thirst that birthed the church a decade earlier.

Jesus wants a bride that is not lying in bed content settling for doctrines and a nice morning service, more worried about not offending the rich tithers than desperately crying out to the living God. Jesus is seeking a bride with the same mindset that love is first. Desperation for Him is first. A bride waiting by the door so that in a moments notice, she senses Him and opens it, or better yet, a bride that stands in the threshold with the door open continuously to the King of glory.

This was actually the prayer of Christ. *John 17:20-21, I do not pray for these alone, but also for those who will believe in Me through their word; that they all may be one, as You, Father, are in Me, and I in You; that they also may be one in Us, that the world may believe that You sent Me.*

True unity is a bride in desperate love, not a group of people coming together and trying to be nice to each other, reaching out to other organizations creating a common human connection, trying to find agreement. That is humanism. True unity is when the bride has the same desperation for the bridegroom as the bridegroom has for the bride. Desperation for the Spirit of God is what multiplies, and it is contagious. That is what I learned in India. No doctrines to entangle the people, no limitations, just flat out burning for the presence of the Holy Spirit.

The warning to the church of Ephesus was that although they did all the right *Christian things,* they left their *First Love, the Person of the Holy Spirit* (Revelation 2:1-4). They were dressed like the bride and looked like the bride to the natural eye, but they were not positioned in the threshold of the door, crying out for the living God. Don't be fooled, no matter how righteous the group looks on the outside, it's the inside of the cup that Christ measures.

## THE SONS OF GOD

David did many things that violated the Law of Moses. He murdered Bathsheba's husband after he committed adultery with her. He became friends with the Philistines who worshipped demonic idols after running crazy in the desert, murdering his fellow Israelites. He stole from many as the head of his gang in the wilderness.

However, never was he a religious pretender. He never tried to appear righteous to any man nor was he afraid of hiding his love for the anointing of the Holy Spirit. He was totally unconcerned with the religious leaders of the day and the systems needed to achieve the Law of Moses. In contrast, he hungered and thirst after the Holy Spirit, and the Spirit in turn made him a mighty man, a giant killer. He was unafraid to undress down to his loincloth, needing to appear righteous for nothing, making himself vulnerable for all to see his desperate love for Christ. He made dancing in the streets before the Lord almost naked synonymous with killing giants. His mighty acts were not the product of appearing righteous to the people like Saul and his concern for popularity.

Instead, David thirsted for the presence of God with all his heart, mind and soul, and prophesied the word of the Lord against giants, cities and nations, having access to the most powerful force in the universe, the heart of God. He made such an impact on God Himself that God prophesied that the coming Messiah would be known as the Son of David and restoring the tent of David would be the Messiah's mission (Amos 9:11; Acts 1:4-8). As David produced many who also killed giants, imparting the love for the presence of God, so too did Christ prophesy the coming of the modern-day giant killers saying *these signs follow the believers, those who are in absolute, desperate love. In my name you will cast out devils, pray in tongues, take up serpents and demonic powers, drink poison and not be harmed, and lay hands on the sick and see them recover (Mark 16:15-18).*

I believe I hear the Lord say, *Like David who dwelled in My presence, prophesying the hearing of My voice and My vision, so too will the modern day giant slayers lay under the shadow of My wing, as desperate for Me as I am for them!*

# ABOUT THE AUTHOR

David is a husband of 28 years to his wife Shelly and is the father of three beautiful children, Baylee, Kamryn and Cole. David is a revivalist at heart and leads a ministry vision that is international, having a ministry organization in India and in the USA.

5 Stones Ministries is a multifunctional organization which focuses on equipping pastors and church organizations in the power of the Holy Spirit, revival, and awakening desperate love of the Holy Spirit in India and the USA. David currently works with church organizations to equip congregations to hear the voice of God and equip leaders to go to the nations. *5 Stones Ministries* has a vision of reaching a million people to be baptized in the Holy Spirit.

*TO CONTRIBUTE AND DISCOVER MORE VISIT:*

**www.5StonesMinistries.org**
**Facebook / 5 Stones Ministries Inc.**

INDIA MINISTRY PHOTOS

Made in the USA
Coppell, TX
20 November 2024

40609967R00105